Nola the Nurse®

English/ Sight Word Workbook for Kindergarten

Volume 4

by Dr. Scharmaine L. Baker NP

Illustrated by Marvin Alonso

A DrNurse
Publishing House

New Orleans, Louisiana

COPYRIGHT ©2016 by Dr. Scharmaine L. Baker and its licensors.
All rights reserved.

No part of this book may be reproduced or transmitted in any form or by any means, electronic or mechanical, including photocopy, recording, or by any information storage and retrieval system without the written permission of the publisher or author except where permitted by law.

For information address A DrNurse Publishing House
2475 Canal Street, Suite 105, New Orleans, La. 70119
www.NolatheNurse.com

ISBN-13: 978-1-945088-08-7
ISBN-10: 1-945088-08-7

Author Contact info:
DrBakerNP@NolaTheNurse.com

www.DrBakerNP.com
www.NolaTheNurse.com

Name _____
Date _____

What Comes After

A → B

I → ☐

D → ☐

L → ☐

F → ☐

T → ☐

H → ☐

N → ☐

R → ☐

X → ☐

Grade

Name _____
Date _____

What Comes After

J → K   B → ☐

P → ☐   L → ☐

K → ☐   T → ☐

N → ☐   R → ☐

C → ☐   W → ☐

Grade

Name _____
Date _____

What Comes After

C → D   Q →

P →   H →

J →   R →

S →   U →

M →   W →

Grade

Name _____
Date _____

What Comes After

B → C   N → ☐

R → ☐   X → ☐

V → ☐   I → ☐

J → ☐   T → ☐

O → ☐   U → ☐

Grade
☆ ☆ ☆
☆ ☆

Name _____
Date _____

What Comes After

D → E   C → ▢

A → ▢   K → ▢

O → ▢   Q → ▢

F → ▢   X → ▢

E → ▢   H → ▢

Grade

Name _____
Date _____

What Comes After

B → C   M → ☐

P → ☐   S → ☐

R → ☐   Y → ☐

V → ☐   C → ☐

T → ☐   J → ☐

Grade

Name _____
Date _____

What Comes After

M → N

C →

A →

E →

G →

N →

U →

X →

L →

I →

Grade

Name _____
Date _____

What Comes After

C → D   A →

X →   W →

S →   K →

V →   Q →

J →   L →

Grade

Name _____
Date _____

What Comes After

N → O

P →

C →

K →

M →

A →

E →

H →

V →

B →

Grade

Name _____
Date _____

What Comes After

H → I   F → ☐

I → ☐   M → ☐

B → ☐   Q → ☐

L → ☐   V → ☐

J → ☐   J → ☐

Grade

Match each animal to the first letter of its name

G

S

D

C

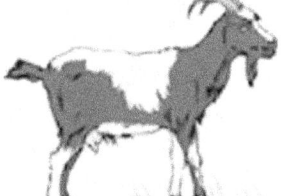

R

Name _____
Date _____

Grade

Name _____
Date _____

Match each animal to the first letter of its name

E

C

D

L

F

Grade

Name _____
Date _____

Match each animal to the first letter of its name

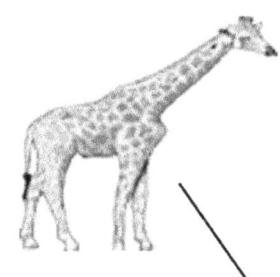

P

C

R

H

G

Grade

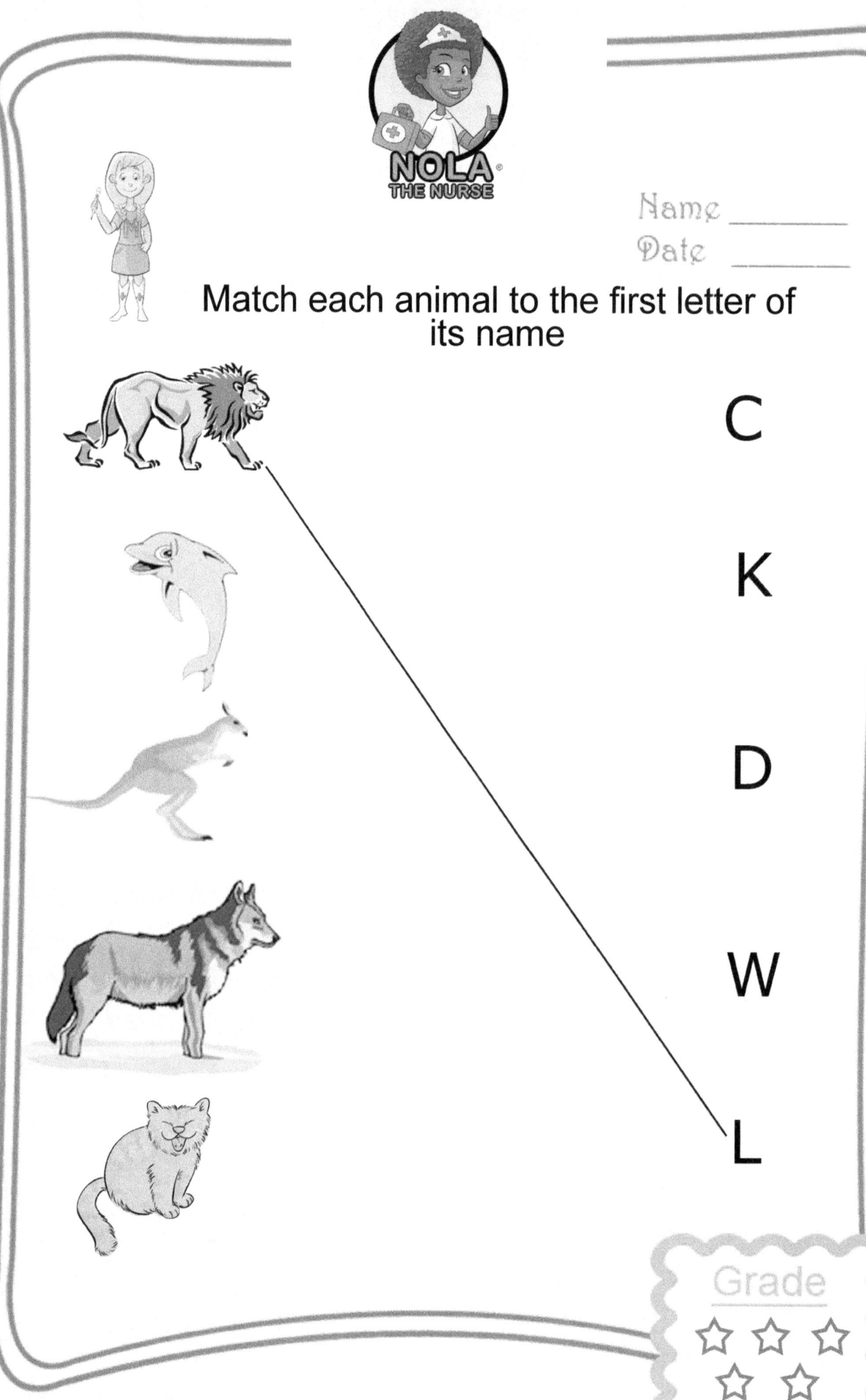

Match each animal to the first letter of its name

C

K

D

W

L

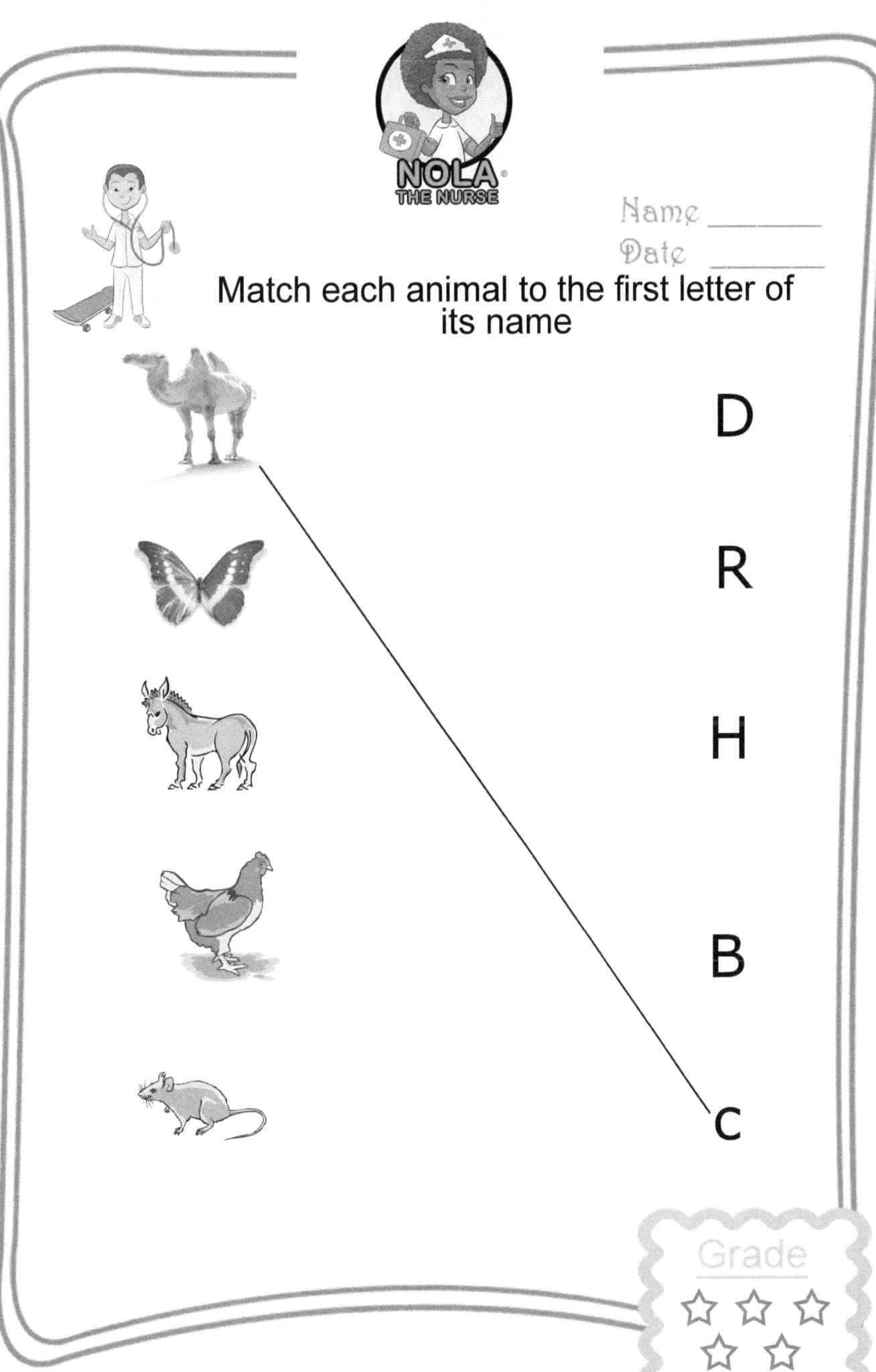

Match each animal to the first letter of its name

Name _____
Date _____

 D

 T

 P

 C

 E

Grade

Name _____
Date _____

Write the Name of each Animal on the Line

 cat _____

 bee _____

 cow _____

 deer _____

Name _____
Date _____

Write the Name of each Animal on the Line

fish   ---------------

frog   ---------------

gorilla   ---------------

horse   ---------------

Grade

Name _____
Date _____

Write the Name of each Animal on the Line

   bear   ---------------

   tiger   ---------------

   butterfly   ---------------

   hen   ---------------

Name _____
Date _____

Write the Name of each Animal on the Line

 elephant ----------------

 dog ----------------

 monkey ----------------

 pig ----------------

Grade

Name _____
Date _____

Write the Name of each Animal on the Line

 rabbit   _____

 rat   _____

 tiger   _____

 lion   _____

Grade
☆ ☆ ☆
☆ ☆

Name _____
Date _____

What Comes Before

B	← C		← H
	← F		← T
	← M		← X
	← Q		← Z
	← J		← U

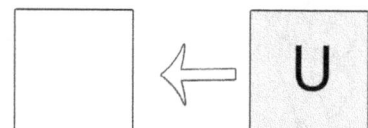

Name _____
Date _____

What Comes Before

Q	←	R			←	P
	←	S			←	L
	←	I			←	W
	←	E			←	U
	←	B			←	T

Grade

Name ____
Date ____

What Comes Before

G	← H		← B
	← F		← N
	← U		← E
	← D		← X
	← R		← S

Grade

Name _____
Date _____

What Comes Before

F	←	G			←	K
	←	P			←	D
	←	R			←	V
	←	W			←	E
	←	M			←	Y

Grade

Name _____
Date _____

What Comes Before

A	←	B			←	D
	←	I			←	S
	←	L			←	F
	←	Q			←	H
	←	P			←	U

Grade

Name _____
Date _____

What Comes Before

D	←	E			←	B
H					←	S
	←	N			←	O
	←	K			←	C
	←	W			←	G

Grade

Name _____
Date _____

What Comes Before

C	←	B			←	G
	←	F			←	N
	←	J			←	S
	←	Y			←	L
	←	T			←	Z

Grade

What Comes Before

Name _____
Date _____

Y ← Z	☐ ← E
☐ ← I	☐ ← Q
☐ ← R	☐ ← U
☐ ← U	☐ ← K
☐ ← M	☐ ← V

Grade

Name _____
Date _____

What Comes Before

L	← M		← R
	← O		← N
	← I		← H
	← E		← T
	← C		← Q

Grade

What Comes Before

D ← E	☐ ← R
☐ ← H	☐ ← M
☐ ← D	☐ ← Z
☐ ← P	☐ ← S
☐ ← J	☐ ← X

Name ____
Date ____

Grade

Name _____
Date _____

Words beginning with the Letter A

____pple   ____irplane

____pricot   ____rm

Grade

Name _____
Date _____

Words beginning with the Letter B

____us ____oy

____all ____anana

Grade

Name ____
Date ____

Words beginning with the Letter C

___ar   ___amel

___at   ___ow

Grade

Name _____
Date _____

Words beginning with the Letter D

___og	___onkey

___rum	___uck

Grade

Name _____
Date _____

Words beginning with the Letter
E

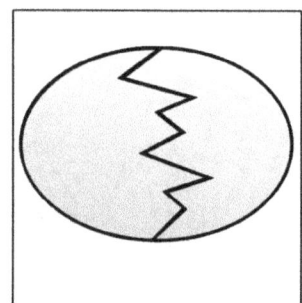

_____
gg

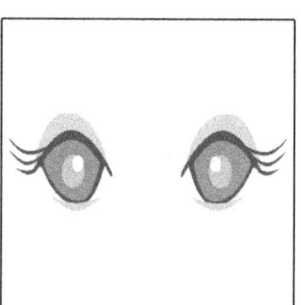

_____
yes

_____
lephant

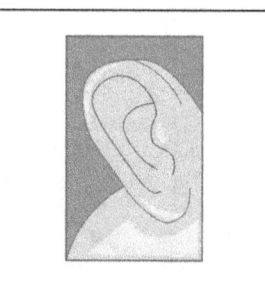

_____
ar

Grade

Words beginning with the Letter F

Name _____
Date _____

____ish   ____ox

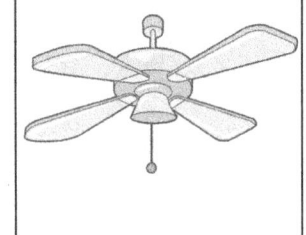

____rog   ____an

Grade

Name _____
Date _____

Words beginning with the Letter G

____rapes   ____un

____irl   ____oat

Grade

Name _____
Date _____

Words beginning with the Letter H

____at   ____orse

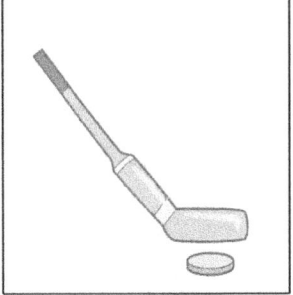

____en   ____ockey

Grade
☆ ☆ ☆
☆ ☆

Name _____
Date _____

Words beginning with the Letter
I

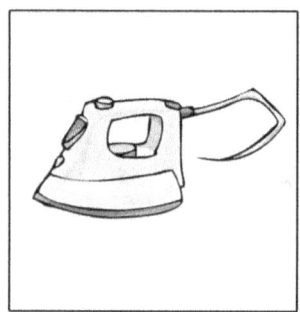

_ron   _gloo

_ce cream   _nkpot

Grade

Words beginning with the Letter J

Name _____
Date _____

___eep

___ar

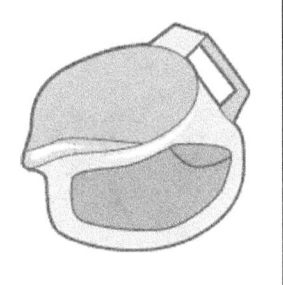

___ellyfish

___ug

Grade

Name ____
Date ____

Words beginning with the Letter K

___ey   ___angaroo

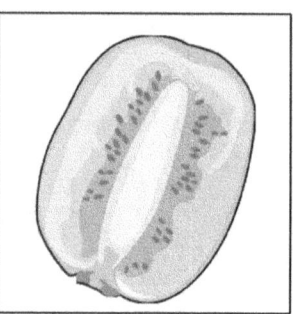

___ite   ___iwi

Grade

Name ____
Date ____

Words beginning with the Letter L

_____ion   _____ock

_____eaf   _____amp

Grade

Name _____
Date _____

Words beginning with the Letter M

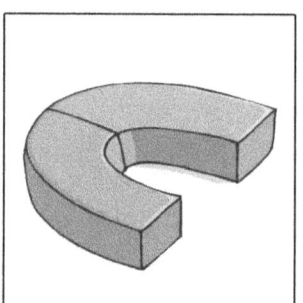

___ ouse   ___ agnet

___ onkey   ___ uffin

Grade

Name _____
Date _____

Words beginning with the Letter N

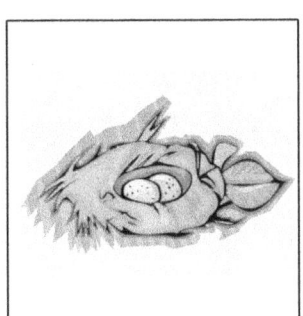

____est   ____urse

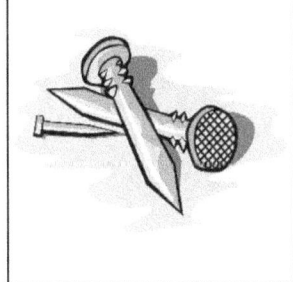

____otebook   ____ails

Grade
☆ ☆ ☆
☆ ☆

Name _____
Date _____

Words beginning with the Letter O

____ctopus   ____range

____wl   ____x

Grade

Name _____
Date _____

Words beginning with the Letter P

____ineapple   ____arrot

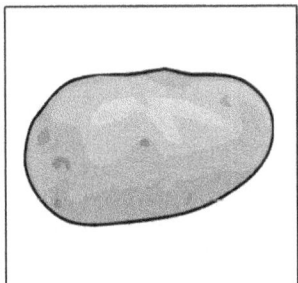

____otato   ____enguin

Grade

Name _____
Date _____

Words beginning with the Letter Q

___uestion   ___uail

___ueen   ___uilt

Grade

Name _____
Date _____

Words beginning with the Letter R

___ose   ___at

___abbit   ___ocket

Grade

Name _____
Date _____

Words beginning with the Letter S

____nake   ____heep

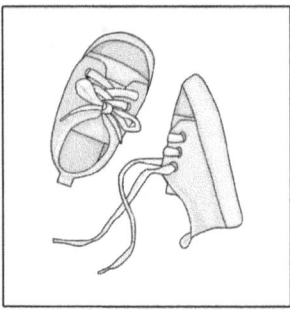

____hoes   ____un

Grade

Name ____
Date ____

Words beginning with the Letter T

_____able   _____iger

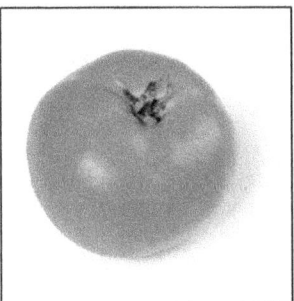 

_____omato   _____eddybear

Grade

Words beginning with the Letter U

Name _____
Date _____

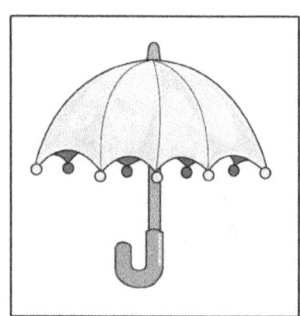

___mbrella ___nicorn

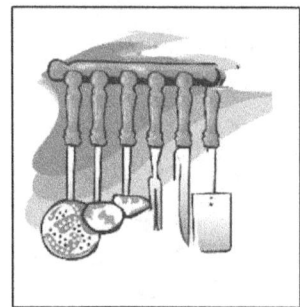

___tensils ___ranus

Grade

Name _____
Date _____

Words beginning with the Letter V

___ an

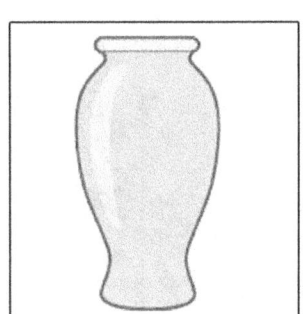

___ ase

___ iolin

___ egetable

Grade

Name _____
Date _____

Words beginning with the Letter W

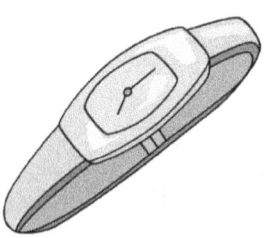
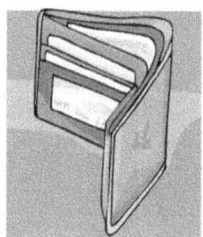

____atch   ____allet

____atermelon   ____alrus

Grade
☆ ☆ ☆
☆ ☆

Name _____
Date _____

Words beginning with the Letter X

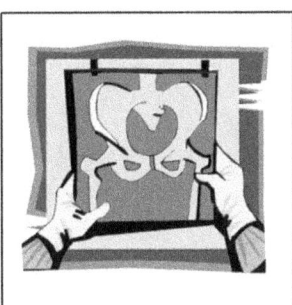

_____
____-ray

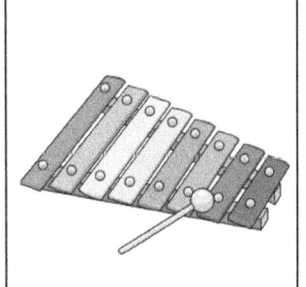

_____
___ylophone

Grade

Words beginning with the Letter Y

Name _____
Date _____

___ak   ___o-yo

___acht   ___ellow

Grade

Name _____
Date _____

Words beginning with the Letter Z

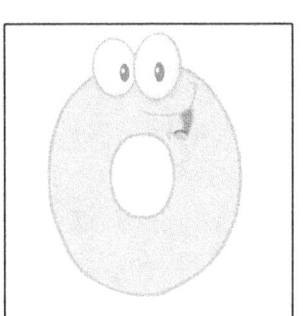

__ebra   __ero

__oo

Grade

Name _____
Date _____

Write the name of each bird on the line

 duck   ----------------

 crane   ----------------

 eagle   ----------------

parrot   ----------------

Grade

Name _____
Date _____

Write the name of each bird on the line

 swan ---------------

 pigeon ---------------

 sparrow ---------------

 woodpecker ---------------

Grade
☆ ☆ ☆
☆ ☆

Name _____
Date _____

Match each bird to the first letter of its name

P

O

H

D

C

Grade

Name _____
Date _____

Match each body part to the first letter of its name

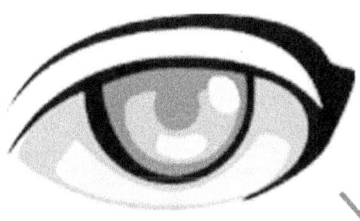   T

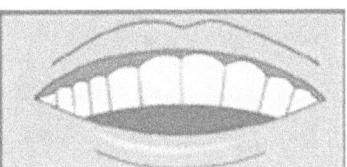   F

   L

   E

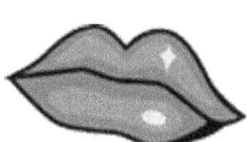   H

Grade

Name _____
Date _____

Match each bird to the first letter of its name

S

P

D

O

W

Grade

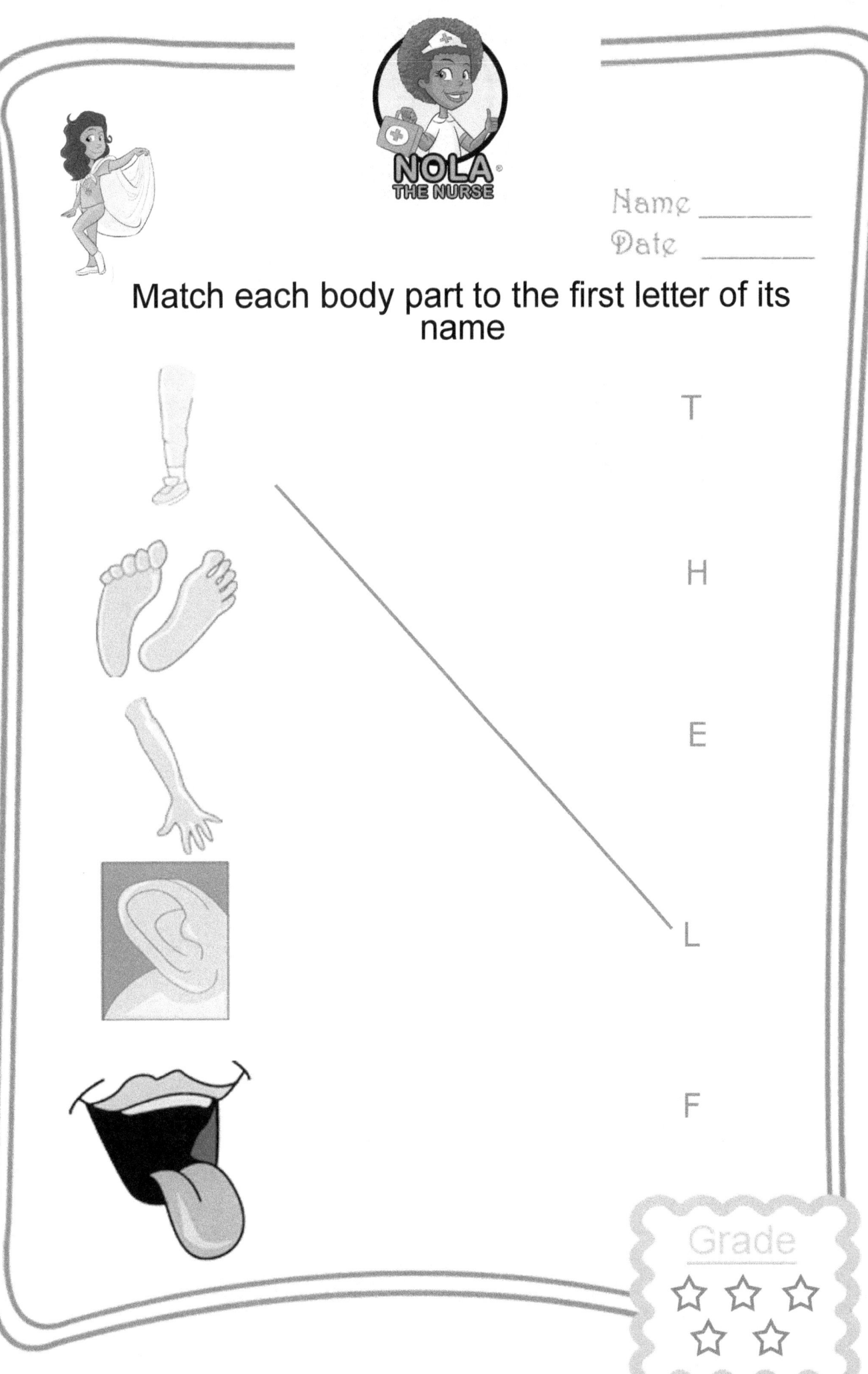

Name ____
Date ____

Match the Body Parts with their names

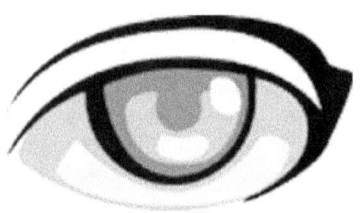	Teeth
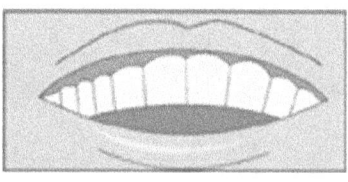	Finger
	Tongue
	Eyes
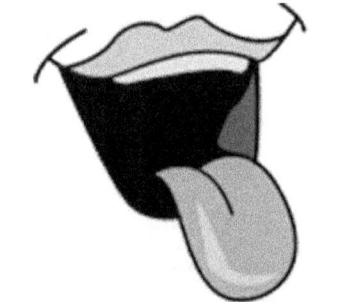	Heart

Grade
☆ ☆ ☆
☆ ☆

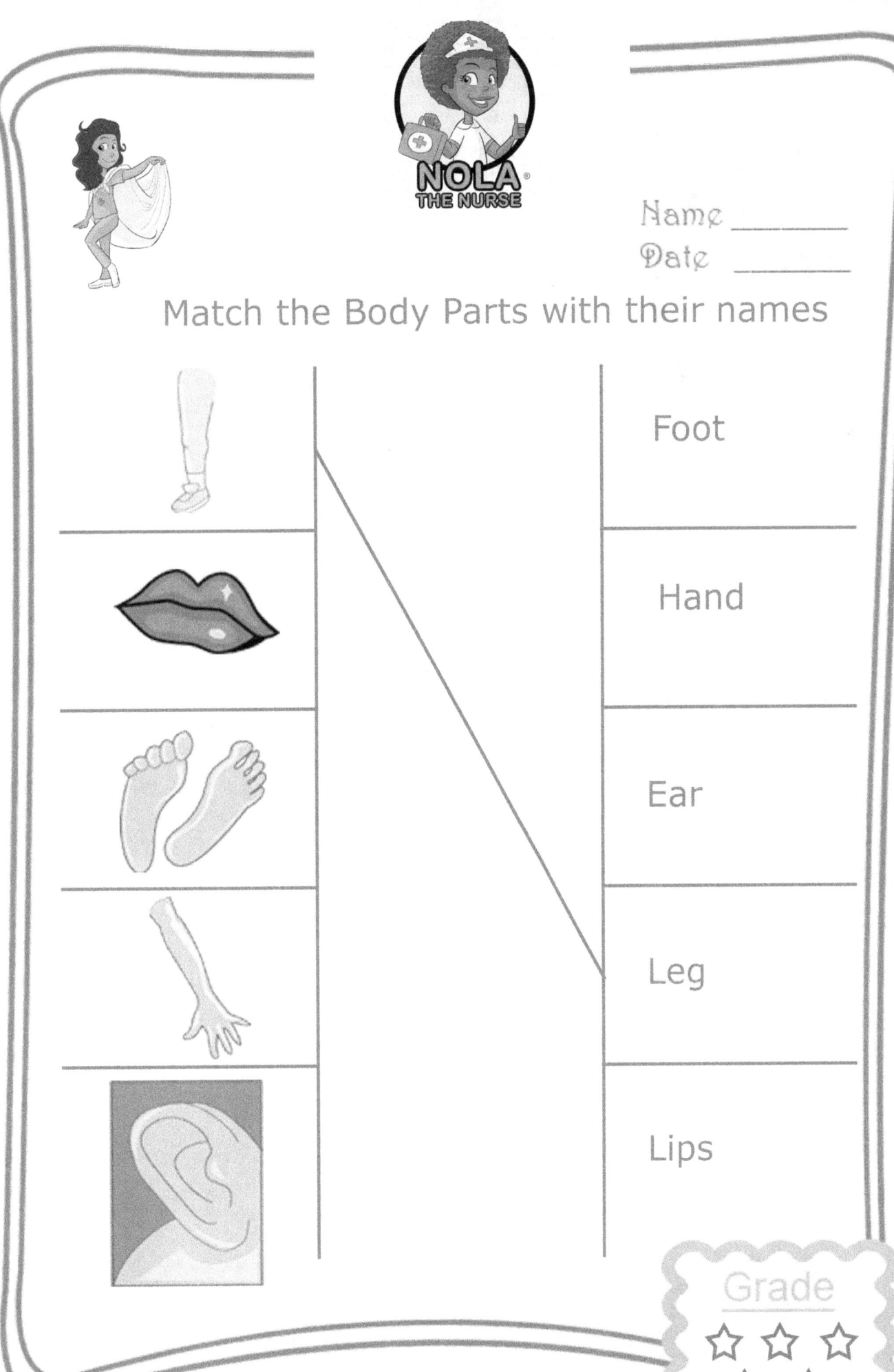

Name _____
Date _____

Dd

Dd Dd Dd Dd Dd

Dd Dd Dd Dd Dd

Dd Dd Dd Dd Dd

Dd Dd Dd Dd Dd

Dd Dd Dd Dd Dd

Grade
☆ ☆ ☆
☆ ☆

NOLA®
THE NURSE

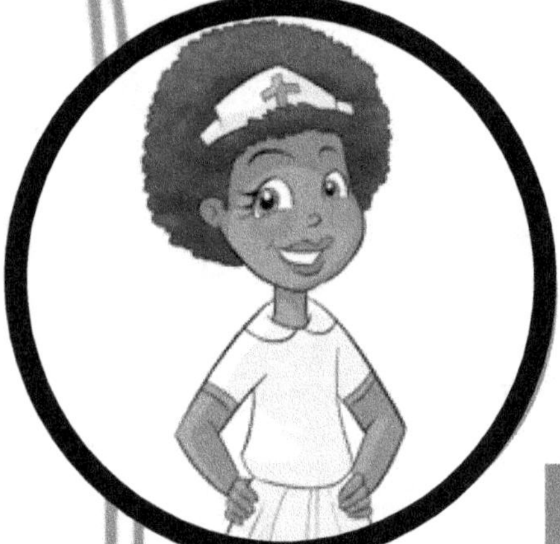

Name ____________
Date ____________

Ee

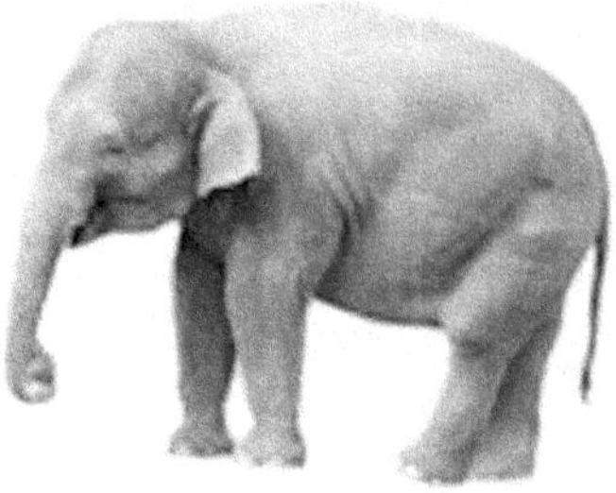

Ee Ee Ee Ee Ee

Ee Ee Ee Ee Ee

Ee Ee Ee Ee Ee

Ee Ee Ee Ee Ee

Ee Ee Ee Ee Ee

Grade
☆ ☆ ☆
☆ ☆

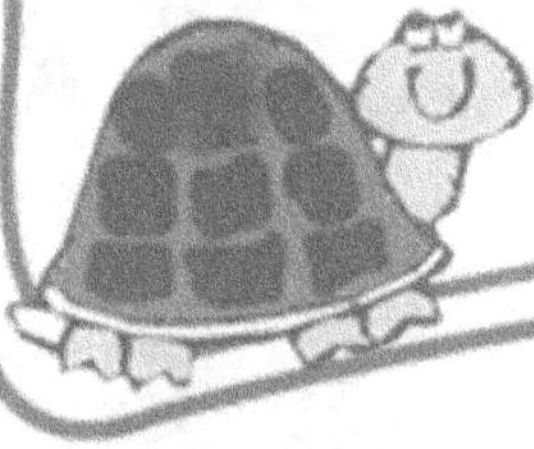

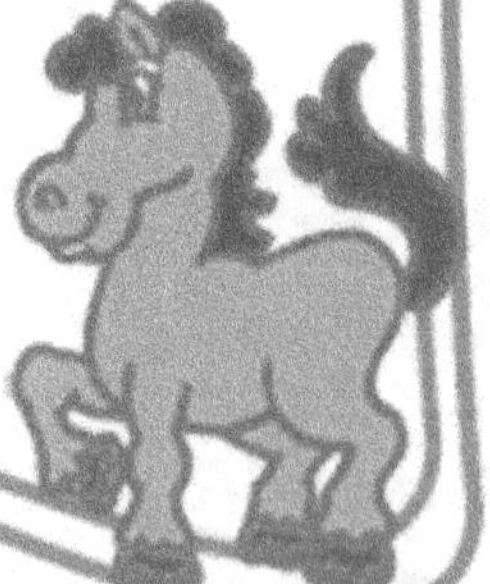

NOLA THE NURSE

Name _____
Date _____

Hh

Grade

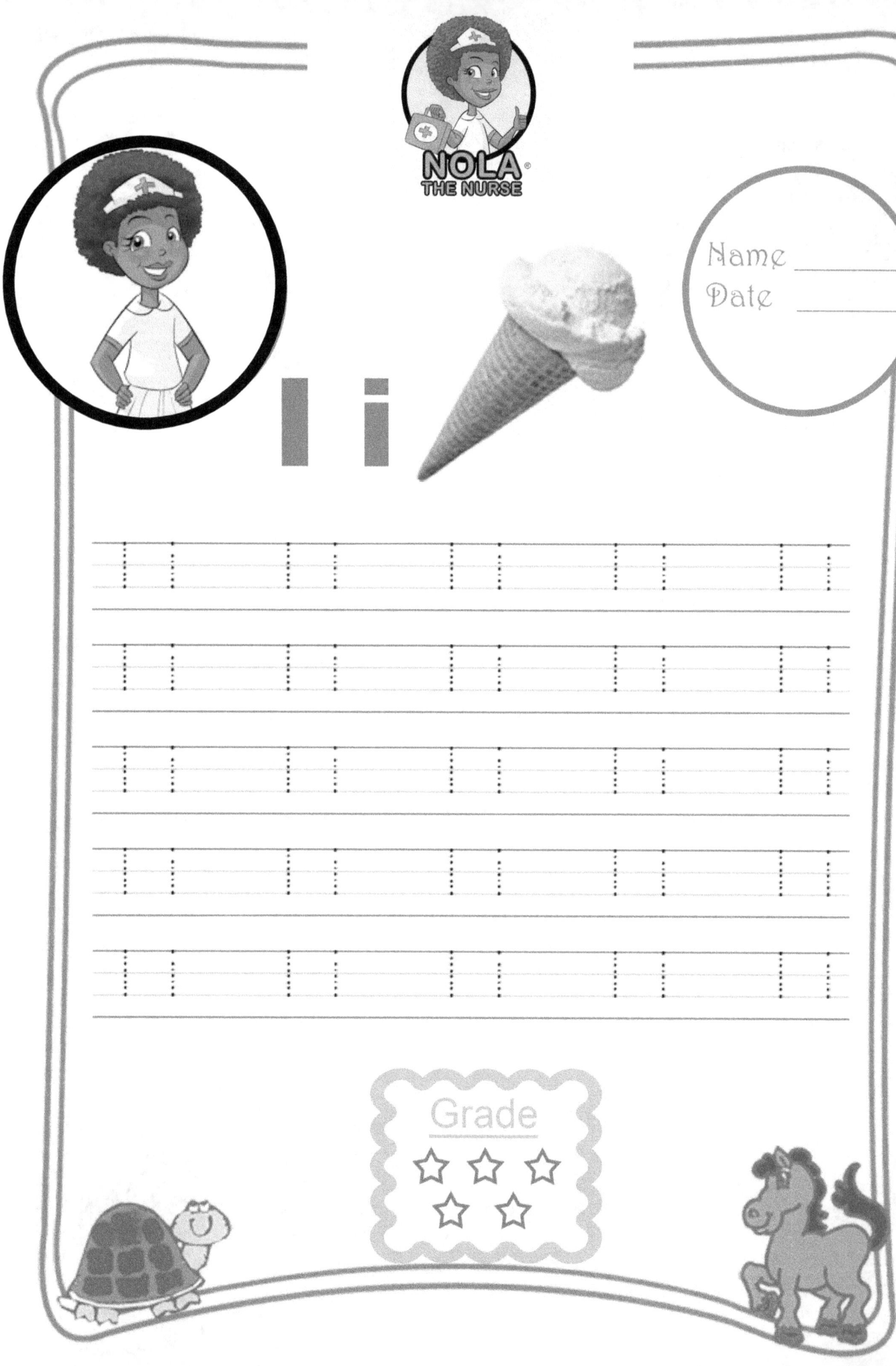

Kk

Name _____
Date _____

Kk Kk Kk Kk Kk

Kk Kk Kk Kk Kk

Kk Kk Kk Kk Kk

Kk Kk Kk Kk Kk

Kk Kk Kk Kk Kk

Nn

Name _____
Date _____

Nn Nn Nn Nn Nn

Nn Nn Nn Nn Nn

Nn Nn Nn Nn Nn

Nn Nn Nn Nn Nn

Nn Nn Nn Nn Nn

Qq

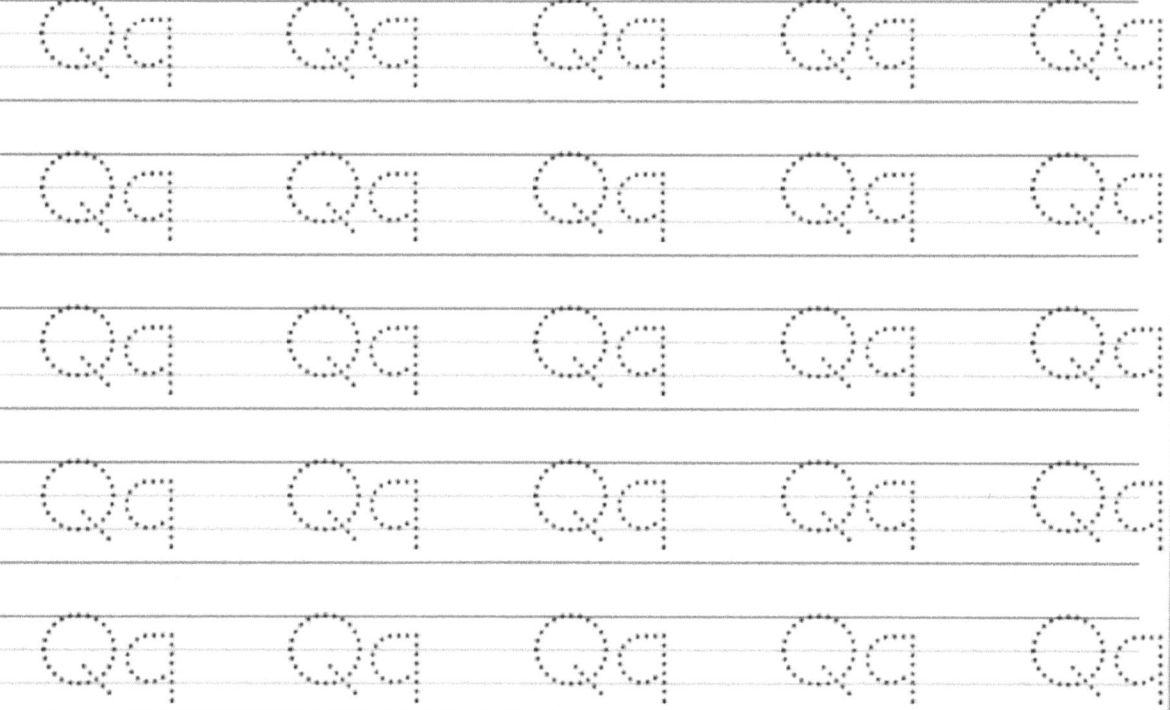

Name _____
Date _____

Grade

Ss

Name _____
Date _____

Ss Ss Ss Ss Ss

Ss Ss Ss Ss Ss

Ss Ss Ss Ss Ss

Ss Ss Ss Ss Ss

Ss Ss Ss Ss Ss

Grade

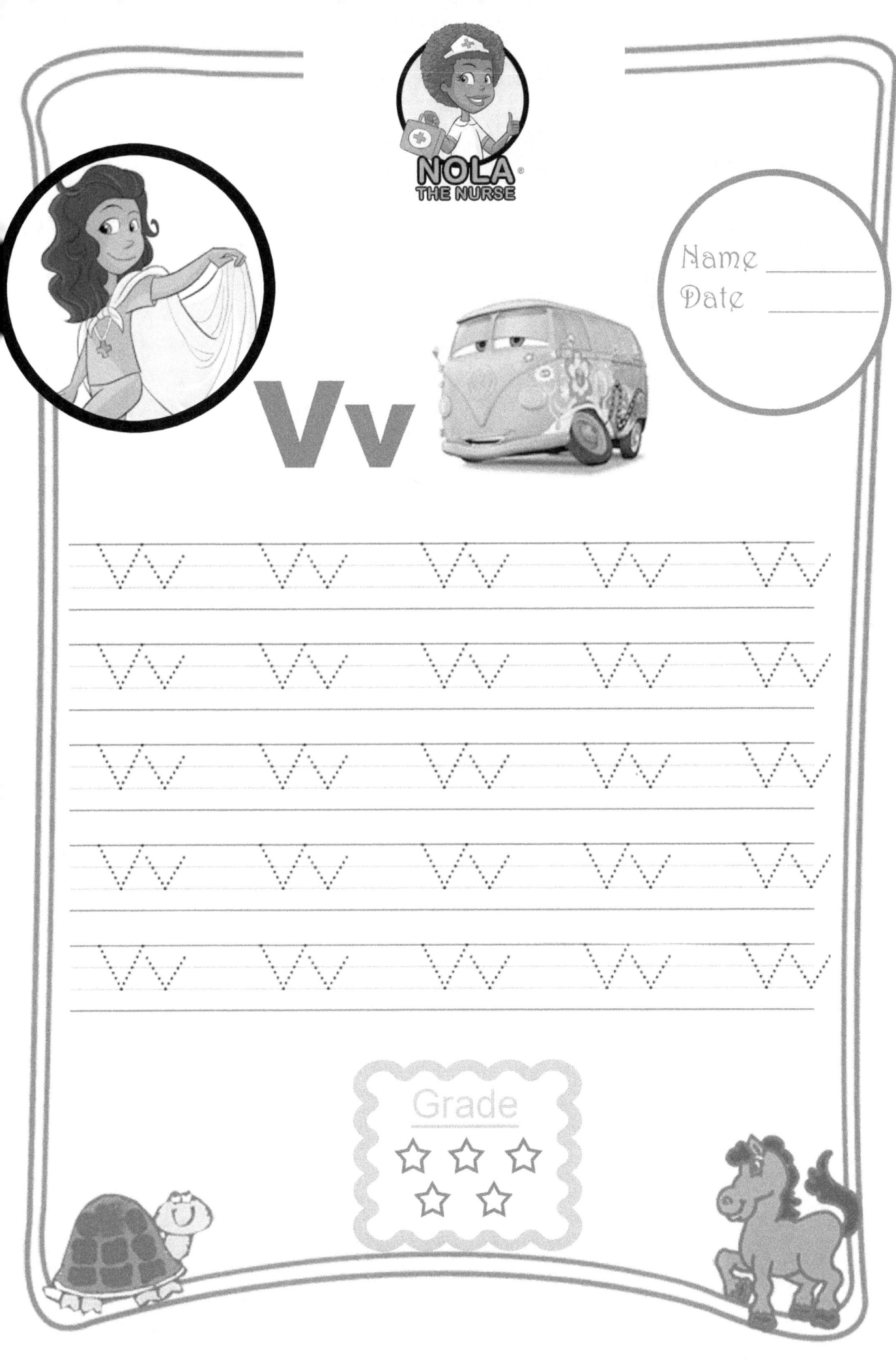

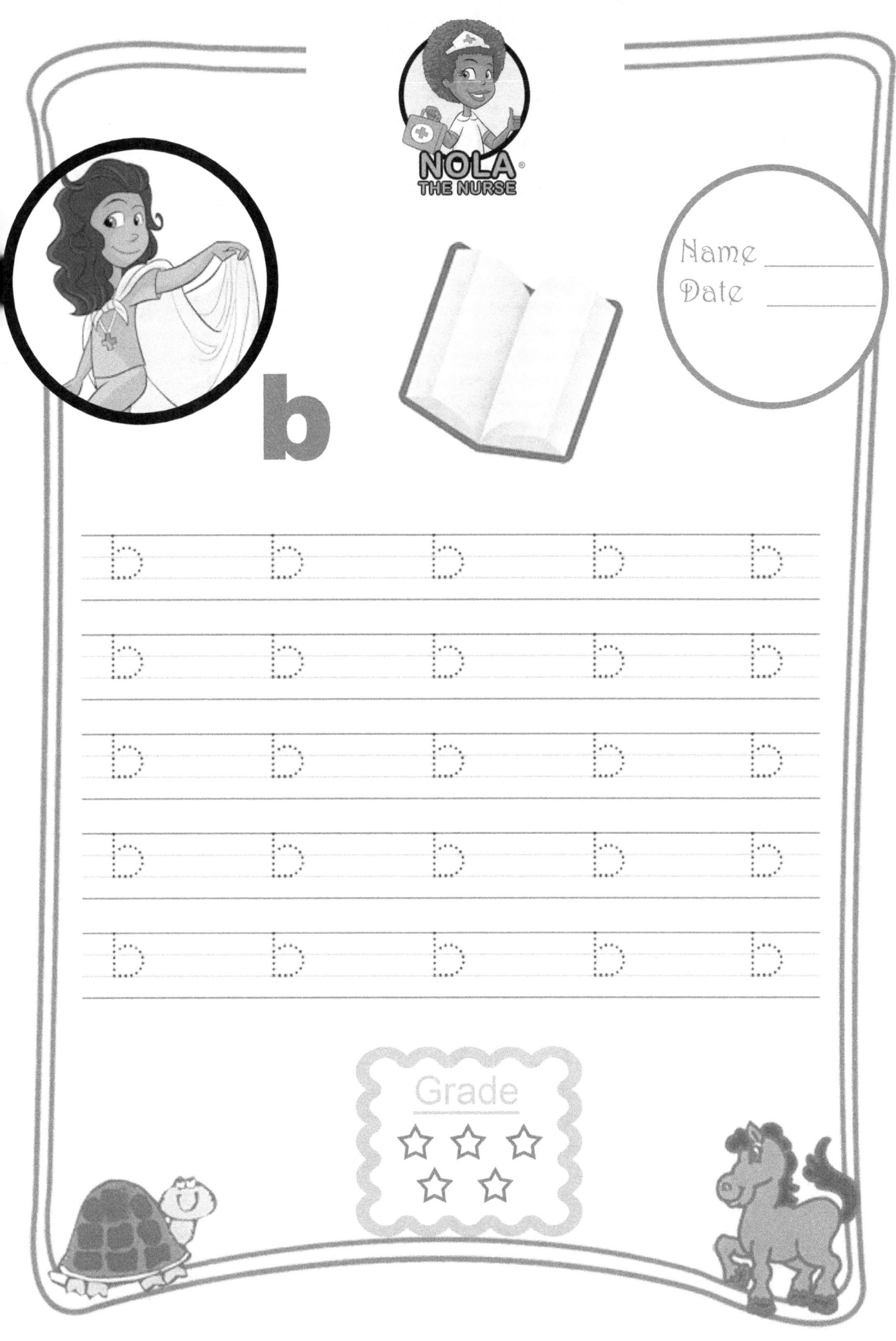

NOLA
THE NURSE

Name _____
Date _____

c

c c c c c

c c c c c

c c c c c

c c c c c

c c c c c

Grade
☆ ☆ ☆
☆ ☆

Name ____
Date ____

e

Grade

f

Name _____
Date _____

Name _____
Date _____

k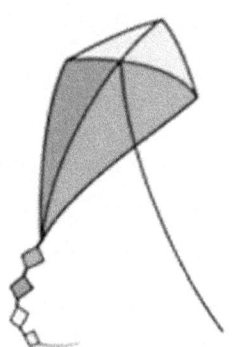

k k k k k

k k k k k

k k k k k

k k k k k

k k k k k

Grade
☆ ☆ ☆
☆ ☆

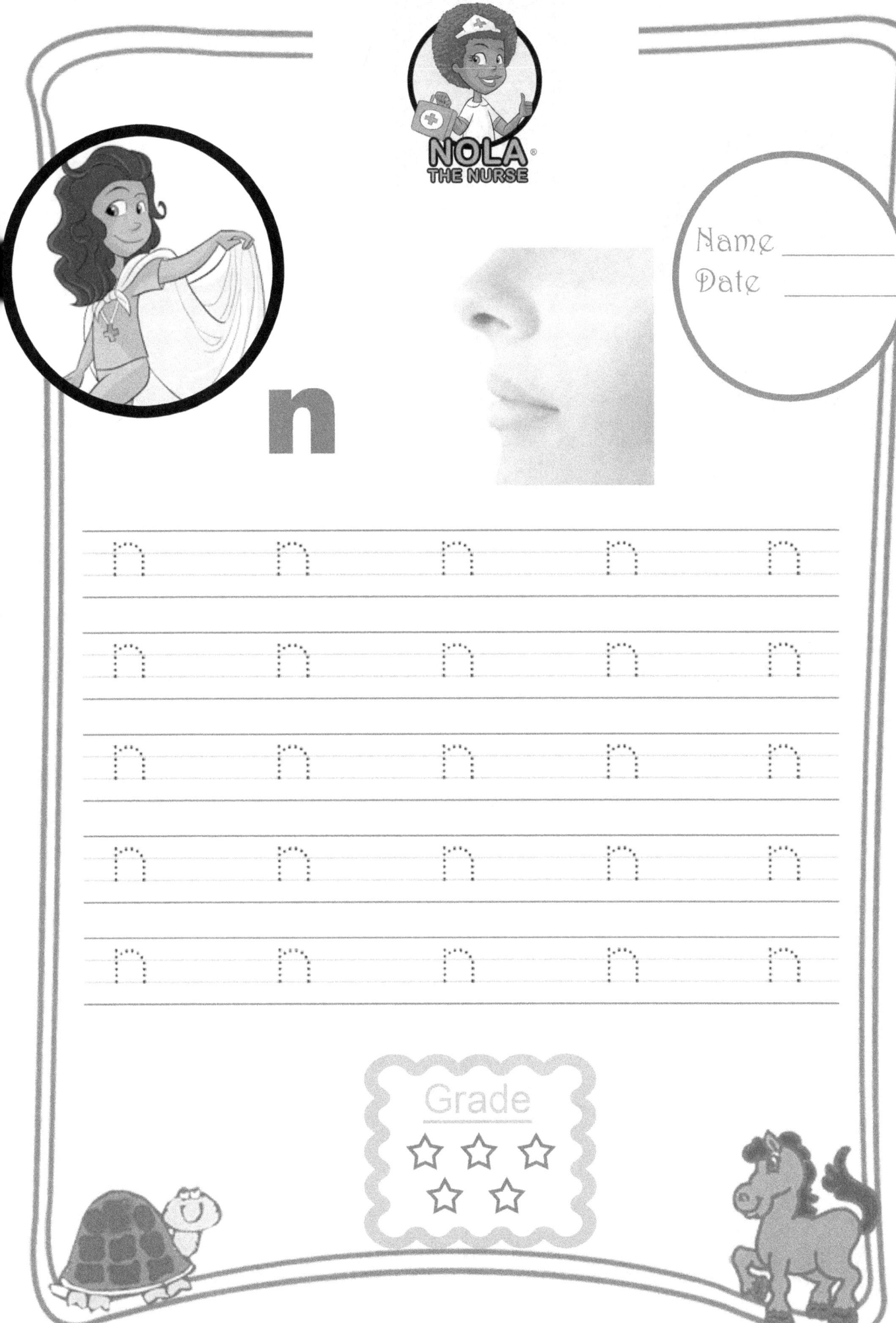

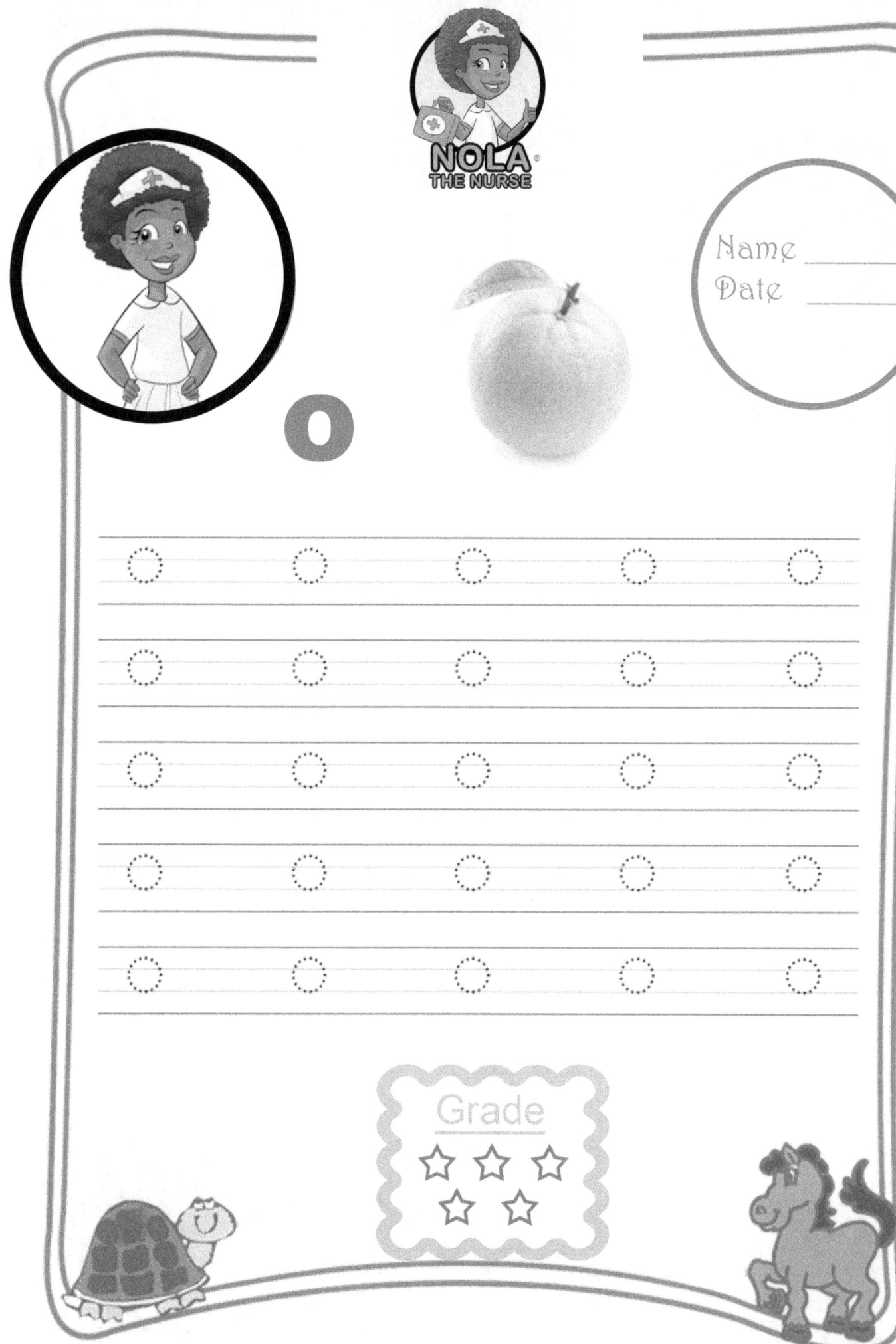

Name _____
Date _____

r

r r r r r

r r r r r

r r r r r

r r r r r

r r r r r

Grade
☆ ☆ ☆
☆ ☆

Name _____
Date _____

s

S S S S S

S S S S S

S S S S S

S S S S S

S S S S S

Grade
☆ ☆ ☆
☆ ☆

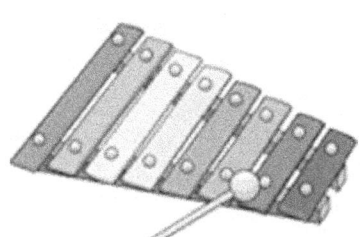

x

Name _____
Date _____

x   x   x   x   x

x   x   x   x   x

x   x   x   x   x

x   x   x   x   x

x   x   x   x   x

Grade

NOLA®
THE NURSE

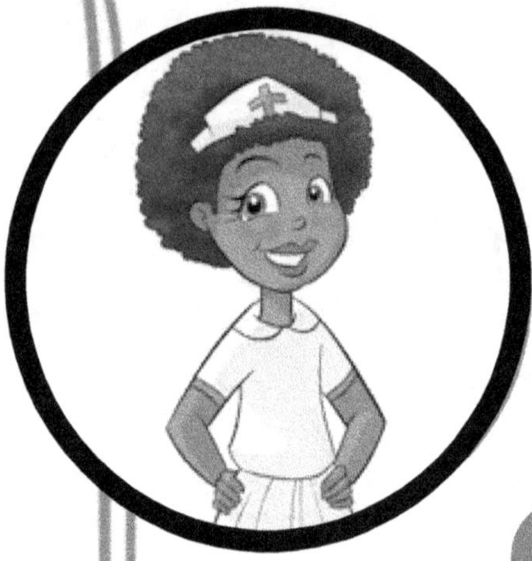

Name ________

Date ________

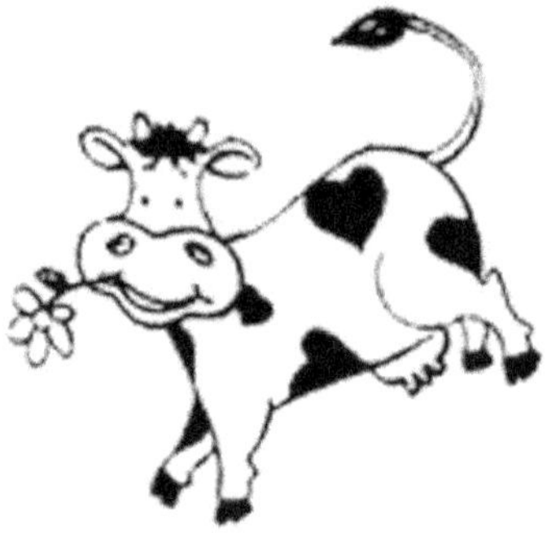

c

c c c c c

c

c

c

c

Grade

☆ ☆ ☆
☆ ☆

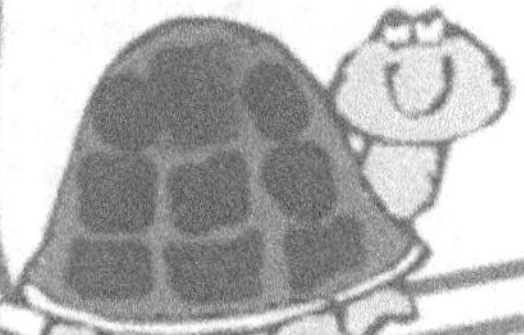

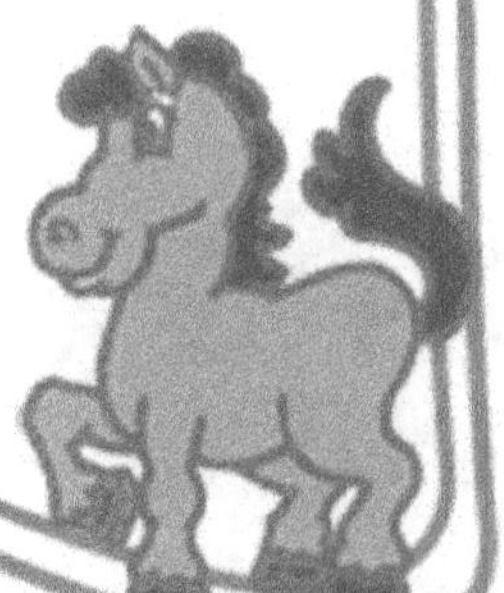

f

f   f   f   f   f

f

f

f

f

Grade
☆ ☆ ☆
☆ ☆

Name _____
Date _____

i

Name _____
Date _____

Grade

Name _____
Date _____

I

Grade

r

Name _____
Date _____

r r r r r

r

r

r

r

Grade
☆ ☆ ☆
☆ ☆

t

Name _____
Date _____

Grade

V

v　v　v　v　v

v

v

v

v

Grade
☆ ☆ ☆
☆ ☆

Name _____
Date _____

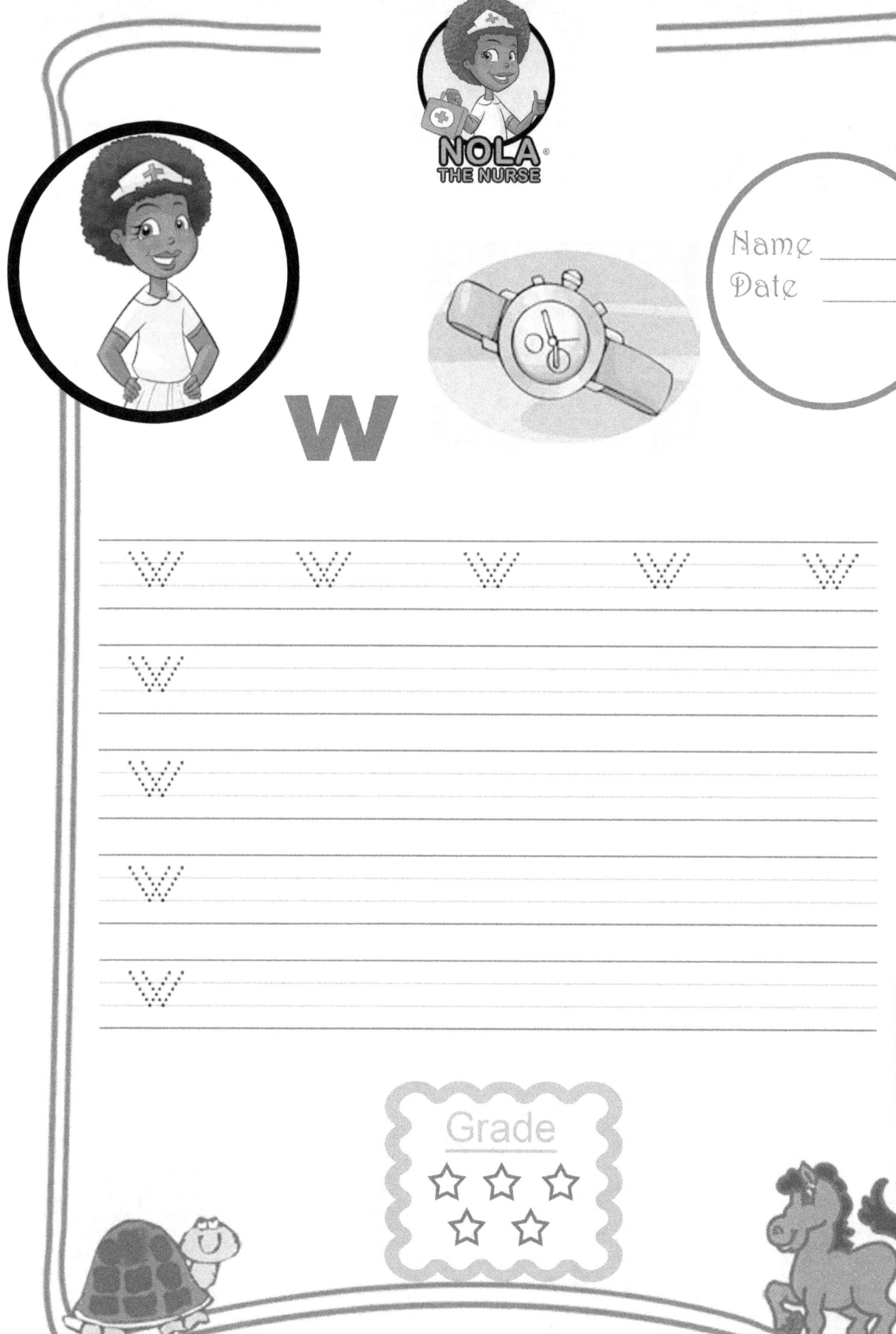

x

Name _____
Date _____

× × × × ×

×

×

×

×

Grade

Name _____
Date _____

a

a	*a*	*a*	*a*	*a*
a	*a*	*a*	*a*	*a*
a	*a*	*a*	*a*	*a*
a	*a*	*a*	*a*	*a*
a	*a*	*a*	*a*	*a*

Grade
☆ ☆ ☆
☆ ☆

Name _____
Date _____

b

b	*b*	*b*	*b*	*b*
b	*b*	*b*	*b*	*b*
b	*b*	*b*	*b*	*b*
b	*b*	*b*	*b*	*b*
b	*b*	*b*	*b*	*b*

Grade
☆ ☆ ☆
☆ ☆

Name _____
Date _____

c

c c c c c

c c c c c

c c c c c

c c c c c

c c c c c

Grade
☆ ☆ ☆
☆ ☆

Name _____
Date _____

d

d	d	d	d	d
d	d	d	d	d
d	d	d	d	d
d	d	d	d	d
d	d	d	d	d

Grade
☆ ☆ ☆
☆ ☆

Name _____
Date _____

e

e	*e*	*e*	*e*	*e*
e	*e*	*e*	*e*	*e*
e	*e*	*e*	*e*	*e*
e	*e*	*e*	*e*	*e*
e	*e*	*e*	*e*	*e*

Grade
☆ ☆ ☆
☆ ☆

Name _____
Date _____

g

g   g   g   g   g

g   g   g   g   g

g   g   g   g   g

g   g   g   g   g

g   g   g   g   g

Grade
☆ ☆ ☆
☆ ☆

h

h   h   h   h   h

h   h   h   h   h

h   h   h   h   h

h   h   h   h   h

h   h   h   h   h

Name ____
Date ____

Grade
☆ ☆ ☆
☆ ☆

Name _____
Date _____

i

i	*i*	*i*	*i*	*i*
i	*i*	*i*	*i*	*i*
i	*i*	*i*	*i*	*i*
i	*i*	*i*	*i*	*i*
i	*i*	*i*	*i*	*i*

Grade
☆ ☆ ☆
☆ ☆

Name _____
Date _____

k

k	*k*	*k*	*k*	*k*
k	*k*	*k*	*k*	*k*
k	*k*	*k*	*k*	*k*
k	*k*	*k*	*k*	*k*
k	*k*	*k*	*k*	*k*

Grade
☆ ☆ ☆
☆ ☆

Name _____
Date _____

m

m	*m*	*m*	*m*	*m*
m	*m*	*m*	*m*	*m*
m	*m*	*m*	*m*	*m*
m	*m*	*m*	*m*	*m*
m	*m*	*m*	*m*	*m*

Grade
☆ ☆ ☆
☆ ☆

Name _____
Date _____

𝓃

𝓃	𝓃	𝓃	𝓃	𝓃
𝓃	𝓃	𝓃	𝓃	𝓃
𝓃	𝓃	𝓃	𝓃	𝓃
𝓃	𝓃	𝓃	𝓃	𝓃
𝓃	𝓃	𝓃	𝓃	𝓃

Grade
☆ ☆ ☆
☆ ☆

Name _____
Date _____

𝒪

𝒪	𝒪	𝒪	𝒪	𝒪
𝒪	𝒪	𝒪	𝒪	𝒪
𝒪	𝒪	𝒪	𝒪	𝒪
𝒪	𝒪	𝒪	𝒪	𝒪
𝒪	𝒪	𝒪	𝒪	𝒪

Grade
☆ ☆ ☆
☆ ☆

Name _____
Date _____

p

p	*p*	*p*	*p*	*p*
p	*p*	*p*	*p*	*p*
p	*p*	*p*	*p*	*p*
p	*p*	*p*	*p*	*p*
p	*p*	*p*	*p*	*p*

Name _____
Date _____

q

q   *q*   *q*   *q*   *q*

q   *q*   *q*   *q*   *q*

q   *q*   *q*   *q*   *q*

q   *q*   *q*   *q*   *q*

q   *q*   *q*   *q*   *q*

Grade ★ ★ ★ ★ ★

Name _____
Date _____

s

| s | s | s | s | s |

| s | s | s | s | s |

| s | s | s | s | s |

| s | s | s | s | s |

| s | s | s | s | s |

Grade
☆ ☆ ☆
☆ ☆

Name _____
Date _____

t

t	*t*	*t*	*t*	*t*
t	*t*	*t*	*t*	*t*
t	*t*	*t*	*t*	*t*
t	*t*	*t*	*t*	*t*
t	*t*	*t*	*t*	*t*

Grade
☆ ☆ ☆
☆ ☆

Name _____
Date _____

$\mathcal{u}$

| $\mathcal{u}$ | $\mathcal{u}$ | $\mathcal{u}$ | $\mathcal{u}$ | $\mathcal{u}$ |

| $\mathcal{u}$ | $\mathcal{u}$ | $\mathcal{u}$ | $\mathcal{u}$ | $\mathcal{u}$ |

| $\mathcal{u}$ | $\mathcal{u}$ | $\mathcal{u}$ | $\mathcal{u}$ | $\mathcal{u}$ |

| $\mathcal{u}$ | $\mathcal{u}$ | $\mathcal{u}$ | $\mathcal{u}$ | $\mathcal{u}$ |

| $\mathcal{u}$ | $\mathcal{u}$ | $\mathcal{u}$ | $\mathcal{u}$ | $\mathcal{u}$ |

Grade
☆ ☆ ☆
☆ ☆

Name _____
Date _____

u

u	*u*	*u*	*u*	*u*
u	*u*	*u*	*u*	*u*
u	*u*	*u*	*u*	*u*
u	*u*	*u*	*u*	*u*
u	*u*	*u*	*u*	*u*

Grade
☆ ☆ ☆
☆ ☆

Name _____
Date _____

W

w	*w*	*w*	*w*	*w*
w	*w*	*w*	*w*	*w*
w	*w*	*w*	*w*	*w*
w	*w*	*w*	*w*	*w*
w	*w*	*w*	*w*	*w*

Grade
☆ ☆ ☆
☆ ☆

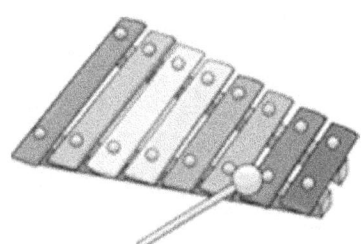

Name _____
Date _____

𝓍

𝓍	𝓍	𝓍	𝓍	𝓍
𝓍	𝓍	𝓍	𝓍	𝓍
𝓍	𝓍	𝓍	𝓍	𝓍
𝓍	𝓍	𝓍	𝓍	𝓍
𝓍	𝓍	𝓍	𝓍	𝓍

Grade
☆ ☆ ☆
☆ ☆

NOLA THE NURSE

Name _____
Date _____

𝒴

𝓎 𝓎 𝓎 𝓎 𝓎

𝓎 𝓎 𝓎 𝓎 𝓎

𝓎 𝓎 𝓎 𝓎 𝓎

𝓎 𝓎 𝓎 𝓎 𝓎

𝓎 𝓎 𝓎 𝓎 𝓎

Grade
☆ ☆ ☆
☆ ☆

Name _____
Date _____

a

| *a* | *a* | *a* | *a* | *a* |

a

a

a

a

Grade
☆ ☆ ☆
☆ ☆

Name _____
Date _____

c

| c | c | c | c | c |

c

c

c

c

Grade
☆ ☆ ☆
☆ ☆

Name _____
Date _____

e

e　　　e　　　e　　　e　　　e

e

e

e

e

Grade

Name _____
Date _____

k

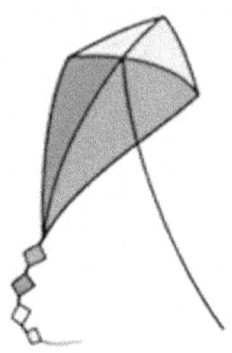

| *k* | *k* | *k* | *k* | *k* |

k

k

k

k

Grade
☆ ☆ ☆
☆ ☆

Name _____
Date _____

m

| *m* | *m* | *m* | *m* | *m* |

m

m

m

m

Grade
☆ ☆ ☆
☆ ☆

Name _____
Date _____

𝓃

𝓃   𝓃   𝓃   𝓃   𝓃

𝓃

𝓃

𝓃

𝓃

Grade
☆ ☆ ☆
☆ ☆

Name _____
Date _____

𝒪

| 𝒪 | 𝒪 | 𝒪 | 𝒪 | 𝒪 |

𝒪

𝒪

𝒪

𝒪

Grade
☆ ☆ ☆
☆ ☆

Name _____
Date _____

q

q   *q*   *q*   *q*   *q*

q

q

q

q

Grade

Name _____
Date _____

s

s s s s s

s

s

s

s

Grade
☆ ☆ ☆
☆ ☆

NOLA®
THE NURSE

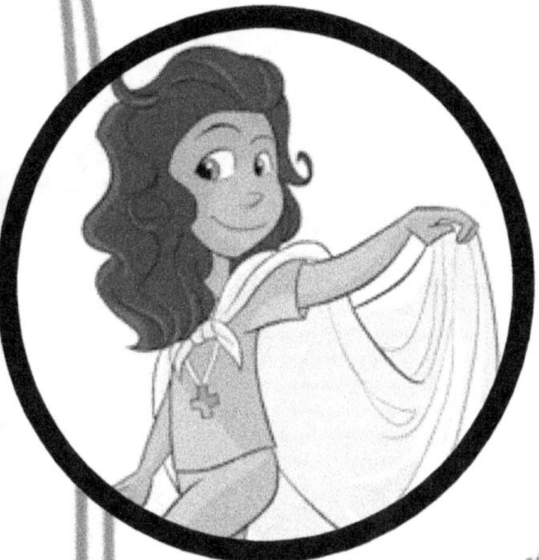

Name ________

Date ________

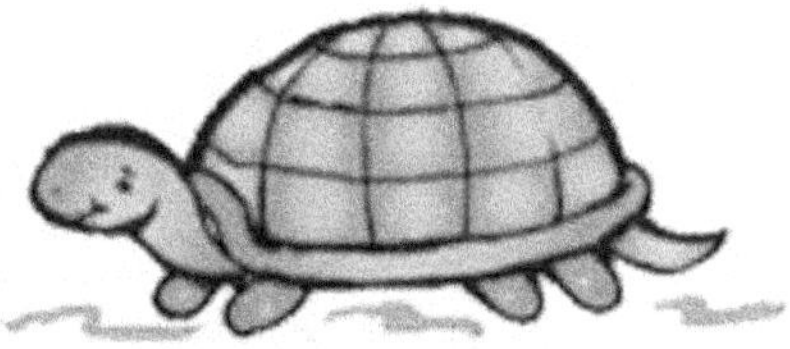

t

t t t t t

t

t

t

t

Grade

☆ ☆ ☆
☆ ☆

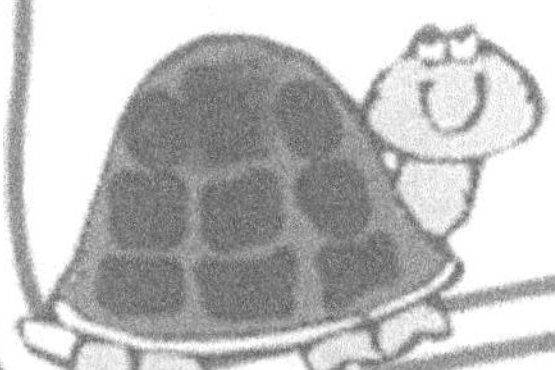

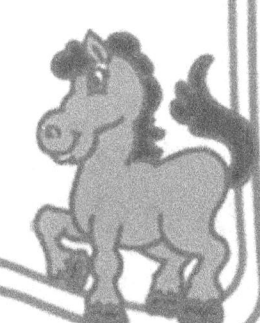

Name _____
Date _____

𝓊

| 𝓊 | 𝓊 | 𝓊 | 𝓊 | 𝓊 |

𝓊

𝓊

𝓊

𝓊

Grade
☆ ☆ ☆
☆ ☆

Name _____
Date _____

𝓊

𝓊 𝓊 𝓊 𝓊 𝓊

𝓊

𝓊

𝓊

𝓊

Grade
☆ ☆ ☆
☆ ☆

Name _____
Date _____

w

w　　*w*　　*w*　　*w*　　*w*

w

w

w

w

Grade
☆ ☆ ☆
☆ ☆

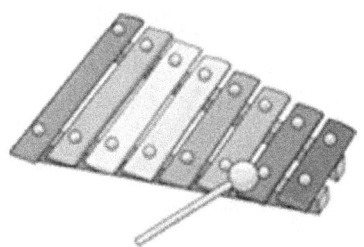

Name _____
Date _____

𝓍

𝓍   𝓍   𝓍   𝓍   𝓍

𝓍

𝓍

𝓍

𝓍

Grade

Name _____
Date _____

a

a   a   a   a   a

a   a   a   a   a

a   a   a   a   a

a   a   a   a   a

a   a   a   a   a

Grade
☆ ☆ ☆
☆ ☆

Name _____
Date _____

B

B	*B*	*B*	*B*	*B*
B	*B*	*B*	*B*	*B*
B	*B*	*B*	*B*	*B*
B	*B*	*B*	*B*	*B*
B	*B*	*B*	*B*	*B*

Grade
☆ ☆ ☆
☆ ☆

Name _____
Date _____

C

C	*C*	*C*	*C*	*C*
C	*C*	*C*	*C*	*C*
C	*C*	*C*	*C*	*C*
C	*C*	*C*	*C*	*C*
C	*C*	*C*	*C*	*C*

Grade
☆ ☆ ☆
☆ ☆

Name _____
Date _____

$\mathcal{E}$

$\mathcal{E}$ $\mathcal{E}$ $\mathcal{E}$ $\mathcal{E}$ $\mathcal{E}$

$\mathcal{E}$ $\mathcal{E}$ $\mathcal{E}$ $\mathcal{E}$ $\mathcal{E}$

$\mathcal{E}$ $\mathcal{E}$ $\mathcal{E}$ $\mathcal{E}$ $\mathcal{E}$

$\mathcal{E}$ $\mathcal{E}$ $\mathcal{E}$ $\mathcal{E}$ $\mathcal{E}$

$\mathcal{E}$ $\mathcal{E}$ $\mathcal{E}$ $\mathcal{E}$ $\mathcal{E}$

Grade
☆ ☆ ☆
☆ ☆

Name _____
Date _____

F

F F F F F

F F F F F

F F F F F

F F F F F

F F F F F

Grade
☆ ☆ ☆
☆ ☆

Name _____
Date _____

g

g   g   g   g   g

g   g   g   g   g

g   g   g   g   g

g   g   g   g   g

g   g   g   g   g

Grade
☆ ☆ ☆
☆ ☆

Name _____
Date _____

𝓗

𝓗	𝓗	𝓗	𝓗	𝓗
𝓗	𝓗	𝓗	𝓗	𝓗
𝓗	𝓗	𝓗	𝓗	𝓗
𝓗	𝓗	𝓗	𝓗	𝓗
𝓗	𝓗	𝓗	𝓗	𝓗

Grade
☆ ☆ ☆
☆ ☆

Name _____
Date _____

𝒦

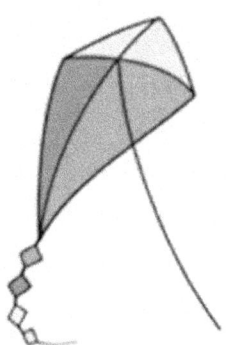

𝒦   𝒦   𝒦   𝒦   𝒦

𝒦   𝒦   𝒦   𝒦   𝒦

𝒦   𝒦   𝒦   𝒦   𝒦

𝒦   𝒦   𝒦   𝒦   𝒦

𝒦   𝒦   𝒦   𝒦   𝒦

Grade
☆ ☆ ☆
☆ ☆

Name _____
Date _____

m

m	*m*	*m*	*m*	*m*
m	*m*	*m*	*m*	*m*
m	*m*	*m*	*m*	*m*
m	*m*	*m*	*m*	*m*
m	*m*	*m*	*m*	*m*

Grade
★ ★ ★
★ ★

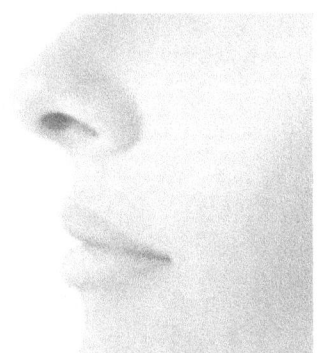

Name _____
Date _____

n

n	n	n	n	n
n	n	n	n	n
n	n	n	n	n
n	n	n	n	n
n	n	n	n	n

Grade
☆ ☆ ☆
☆ ☆

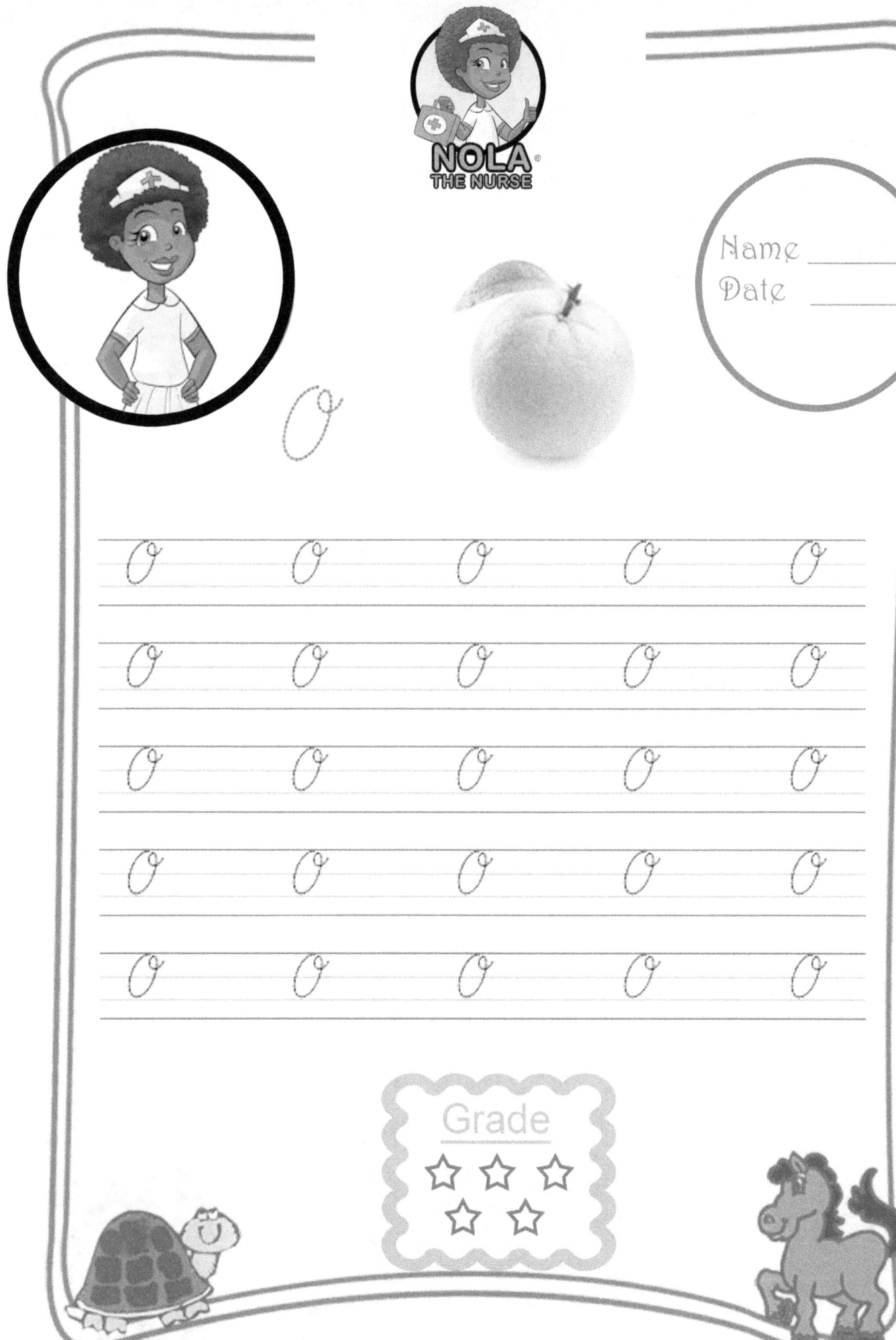

Name _____
Date _____

Q

| *Q* | *Q* | *Q* | *Q* | *Q* |

| *Q* | *Q* | *Q* | *Q* | *Q* |

| *Q* | *Q* | *Q* | *Q* | *Q* |

| *Q* | *Q* | *Q* | *Q* | *Q* |

| *Q* | *Q* | *Q* | *Q* | *Q* |

Grade
☆ ☆ ☆
☆ ☆

Name _____
Date _____

T T T T T
T T T T T
T T T T T
T T T T T
T T T T T

Grade
☆ ☆ ☆
☆ ☆

Name _____
Date _____

$\mathcal{U}$

$\mathcal{U}$ $\mathcal{U}$ $\mathcal{U}$ $\mathcal{U}$ $\mathcal{U}$

$\mathcal{U}$ $\mathcal{U}$ $\mathcal{U}$ $\mathcal{U}$ $\mathcal{U}$

$\mathcal{U}$ $\mathcal{U}$ $\mathcal{U}$ $\mathcal{U}$ $\mathcal{U}$

$\mathcal{U}$ $\mathcal{U}$ $\mathcal{U}$ $\mathcal{U}$ $\mathcal{U}$

$\mathcal{U}$ $\mathcal{U}$ $\mathcal{U}$ $\mathcal{U}$ $\mathcal{U}$

Grade ☆ ☆ ☆ ☆ ☆

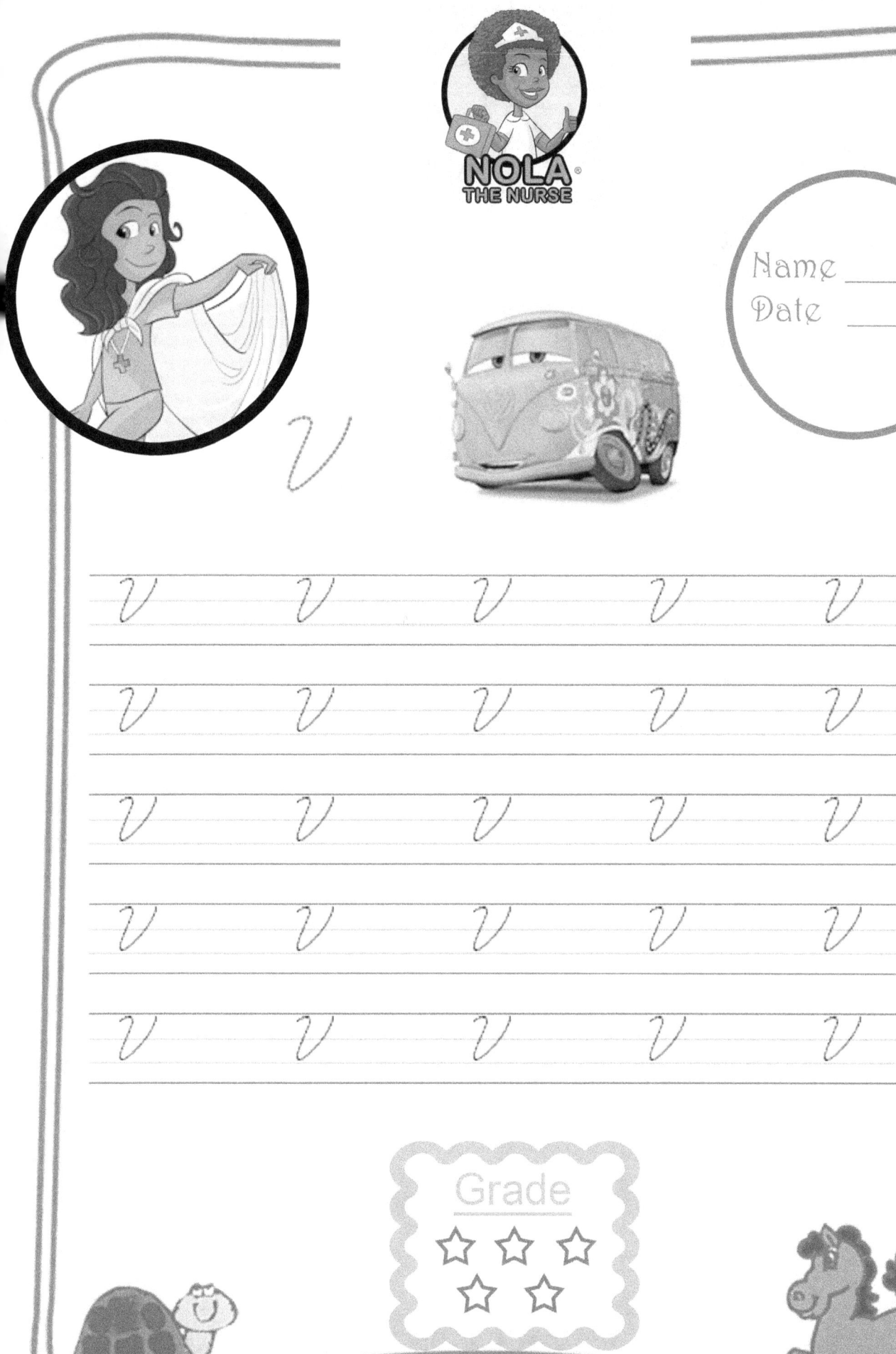

Name _____
Date _____

𝒲

𝒲	𝒲	𝒲	𝒲	𝒲
𝒲	𝒲	𝒲	𝒲	𝒲
𝒲	𝒲	𝒲	𝒲	𝒲
𝒲	𝒲	𝒲	𝒲	𝒲
𝒲	𝒲	𝒲	𝒲	𝒲

Grade
☆ ☆ ☆
☆ ☆

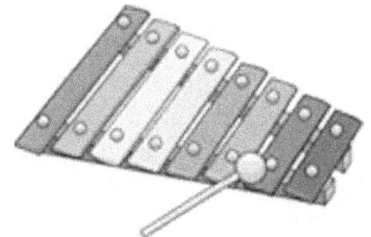

𝓍

Name _____
Date _____

𝓍   𝓍   𝓍   𝓍   𝓍

𝓍   𝓍   𝓍   𝓍   𝓍

𝓍   𝓍   𝓍   𝓍   𝓍

𝓍   𝓍   𝓍   𝓍   𝓍

𝓍   𝓍   𝓍   𝓍   𝓍

Grade
☆ ☆ ☆
☆ ☆

Name _____
Date _____

Match the Animals with their names

   Cat

   Cow

   Goat

   Dog

   Sheep

Grade

Name _____
Date _____

Match the Animals with their names

	Parrot
	Rat
	Bee
	Pigeon
	Rabbit

Grade ☆☆☆ ☆☆

Name _____
Date _____

Match the Flower with their names

		Sunflower
		Rose
		Tulip
		Daisy
		Lily

Grade

Name _____
Date _____

Match each flower to its name

	Pansy
	Marigold
	Bellflower
	Dahlia
	Orchid

Name _____
Date _____

Match the Fruits with their names

	Banana
	Grapes
	Pineapple
	Apple
	Coconut

Name _____
Date _____

Match the Fruits with their names

	Pomegranate
	Strawberry
	Orange
	Pear
	Cherry

Name _____
Date _____

Match the Fruits with their names

		Orange
		Peach
		Melon
		Apricot
		Plum

Grade

Name _____
Date _____

Match each fruit to the first letter of its name

   B

   G

   P

   A

   C

Grade

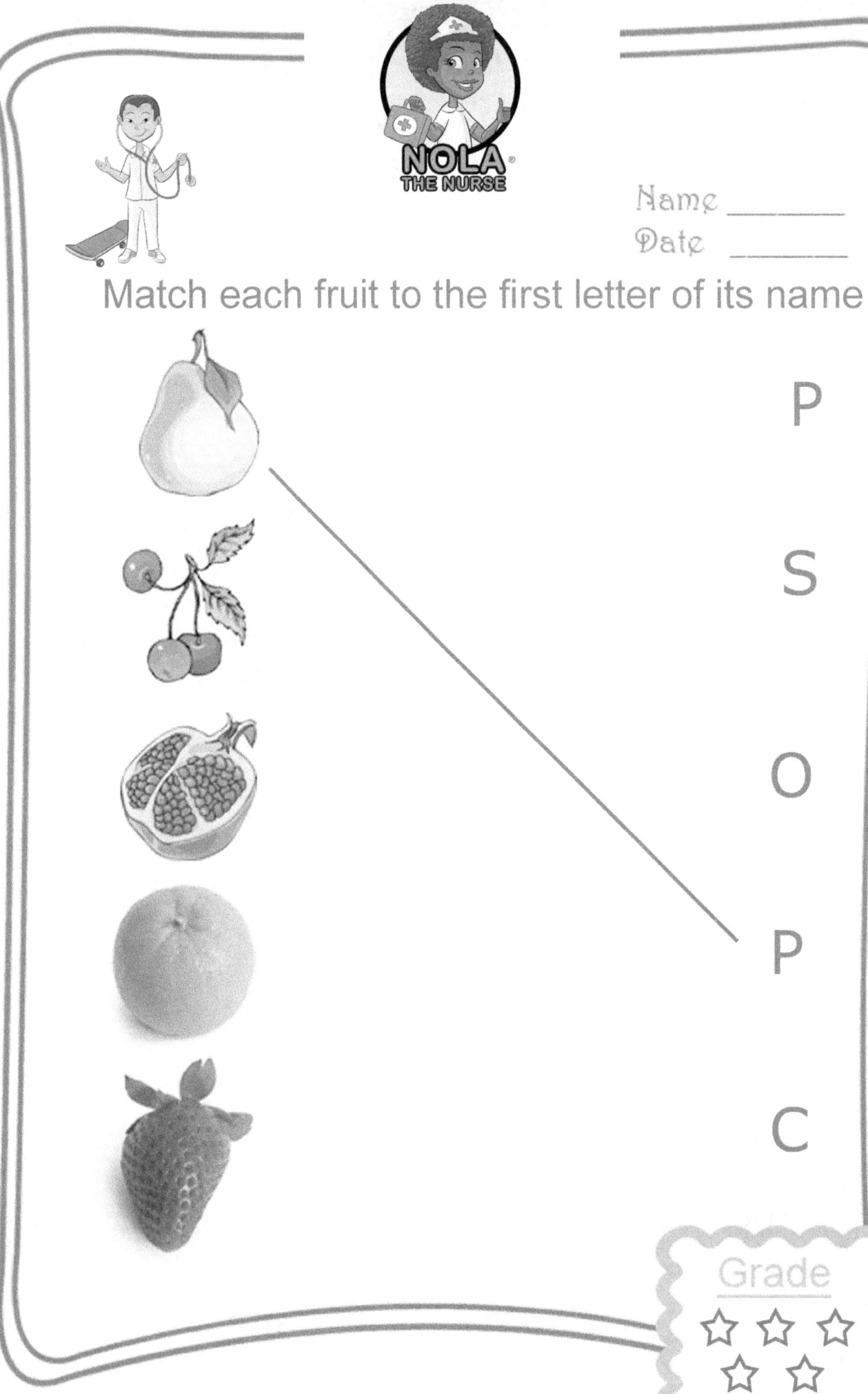

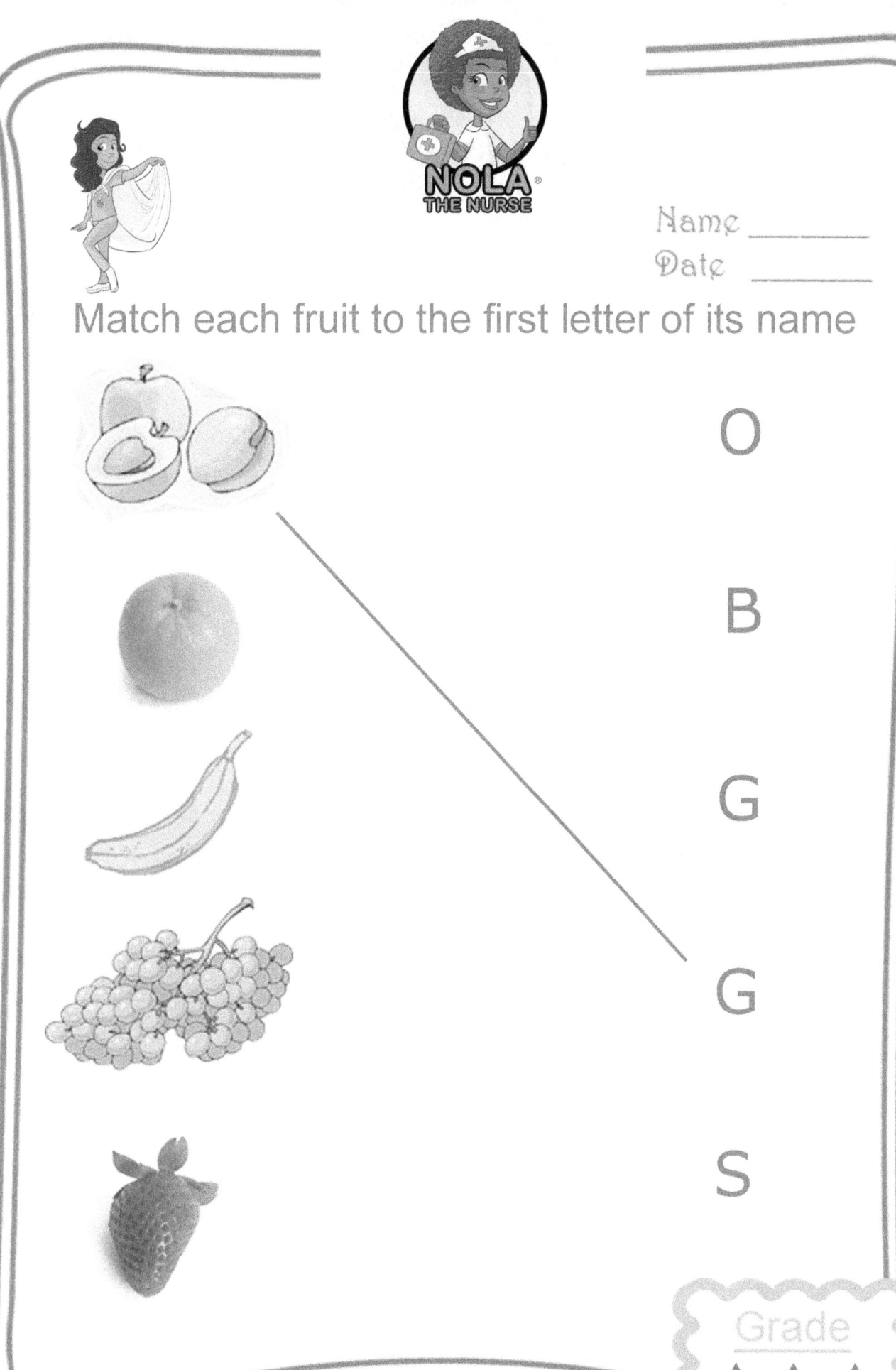

Name _____
Date _____

Match each household item to the first letter of its name

S

B

N

B

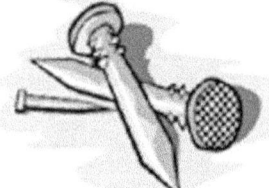

P

Grade

NOLA
THE NURSE

Name _____
Date _____

Match each household item to the first letter of its name

P

C

V

B

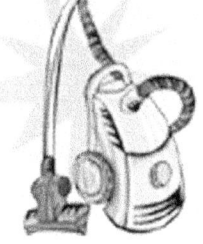

M

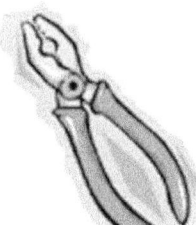

Grade

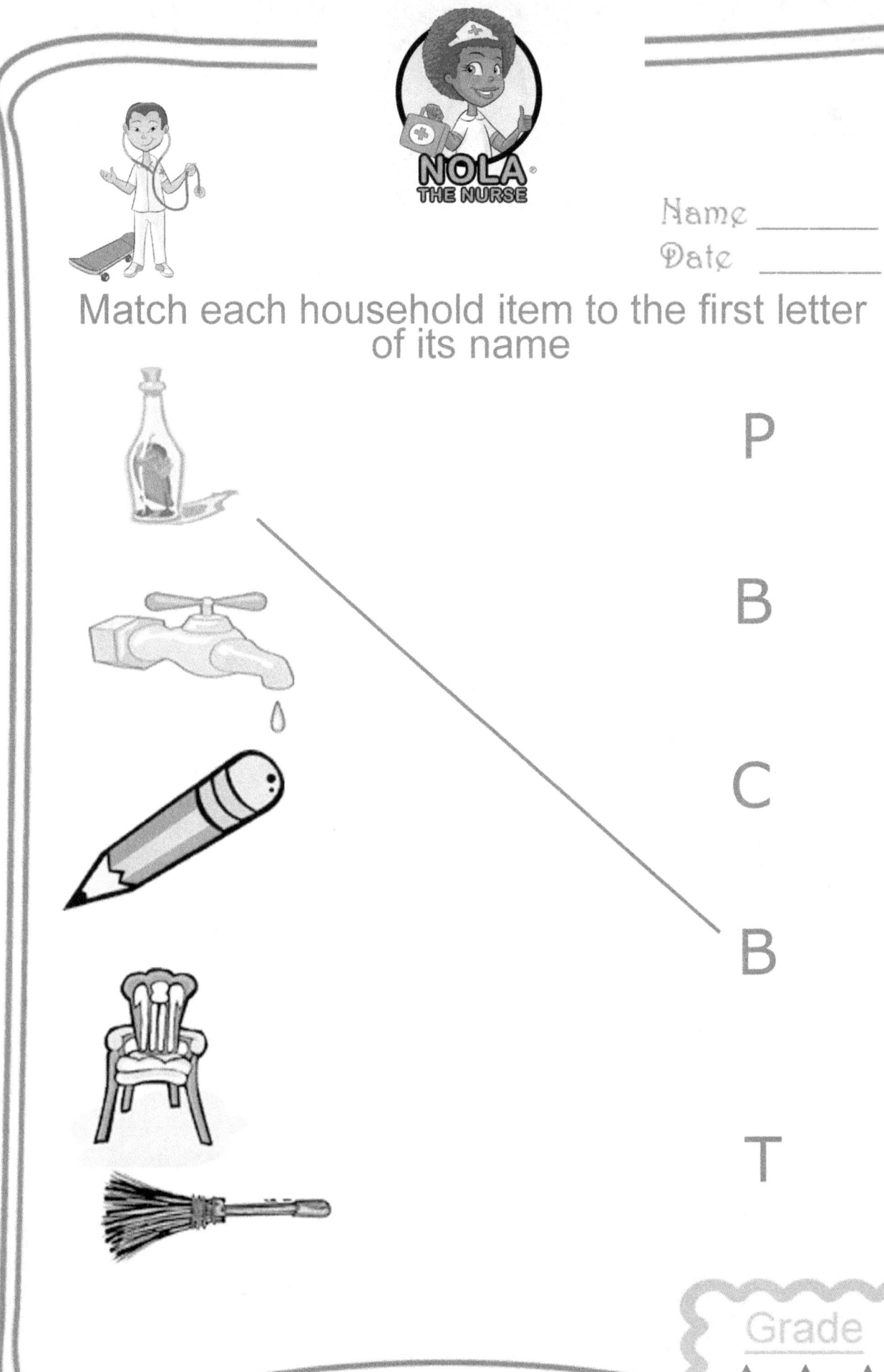

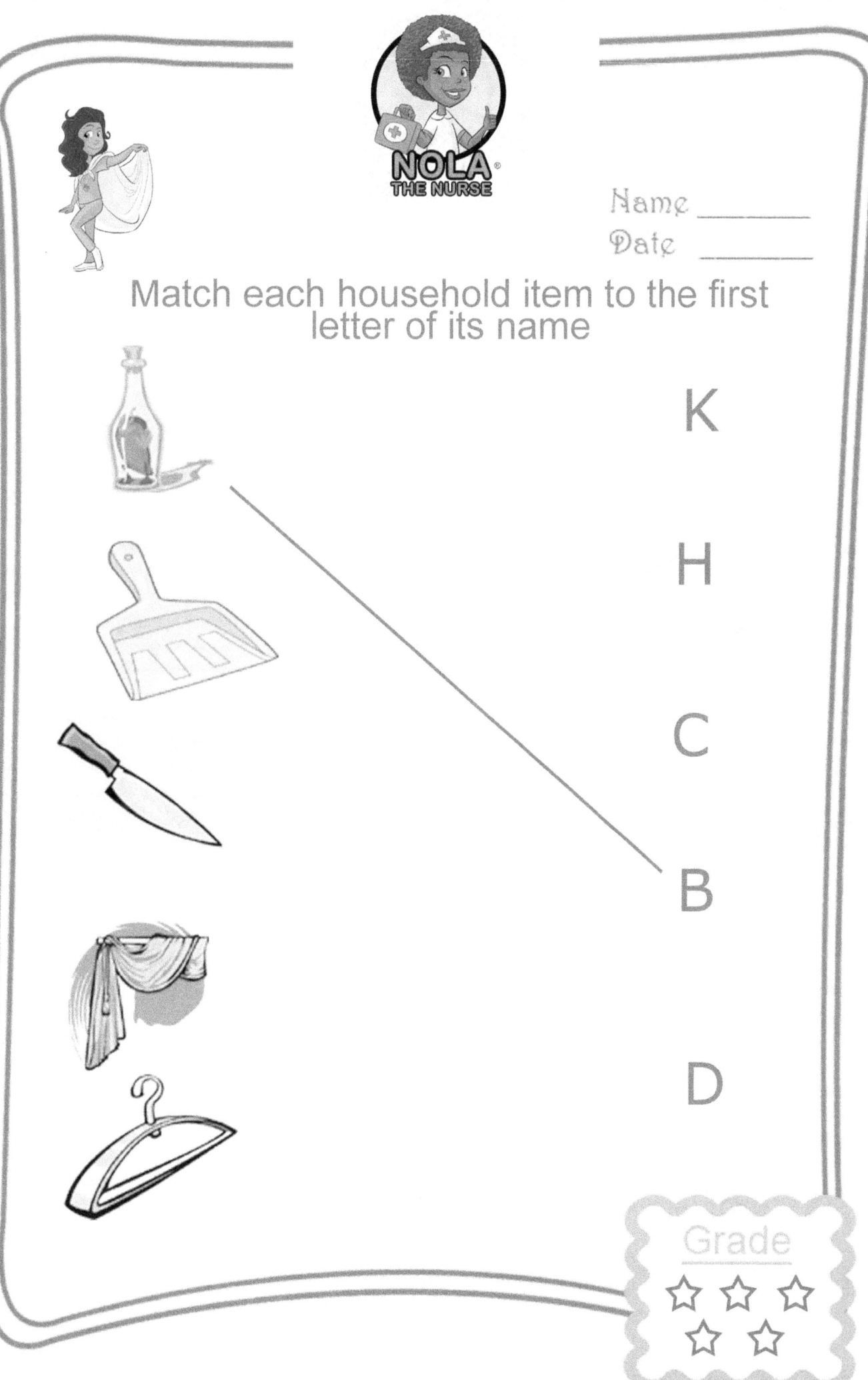

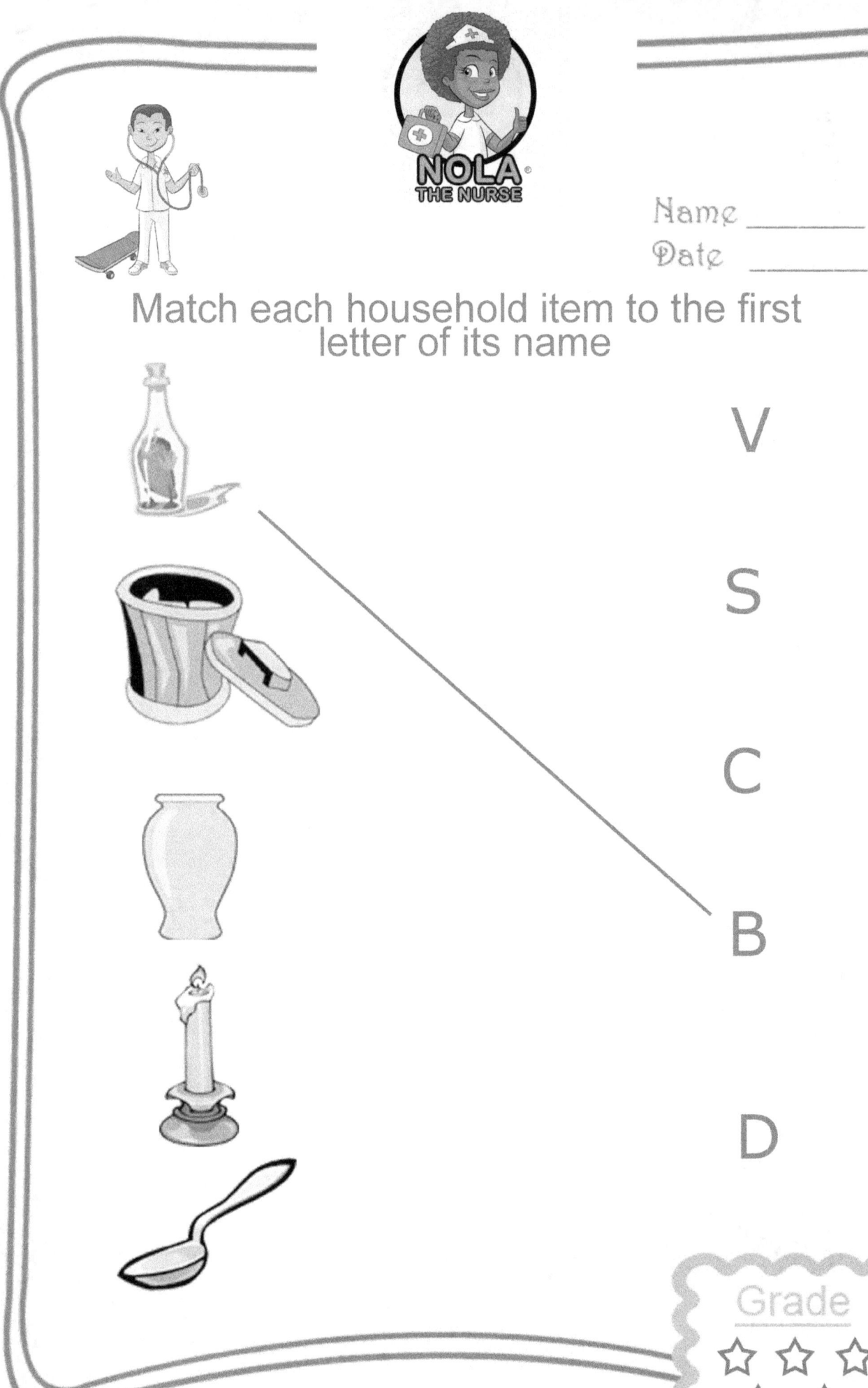

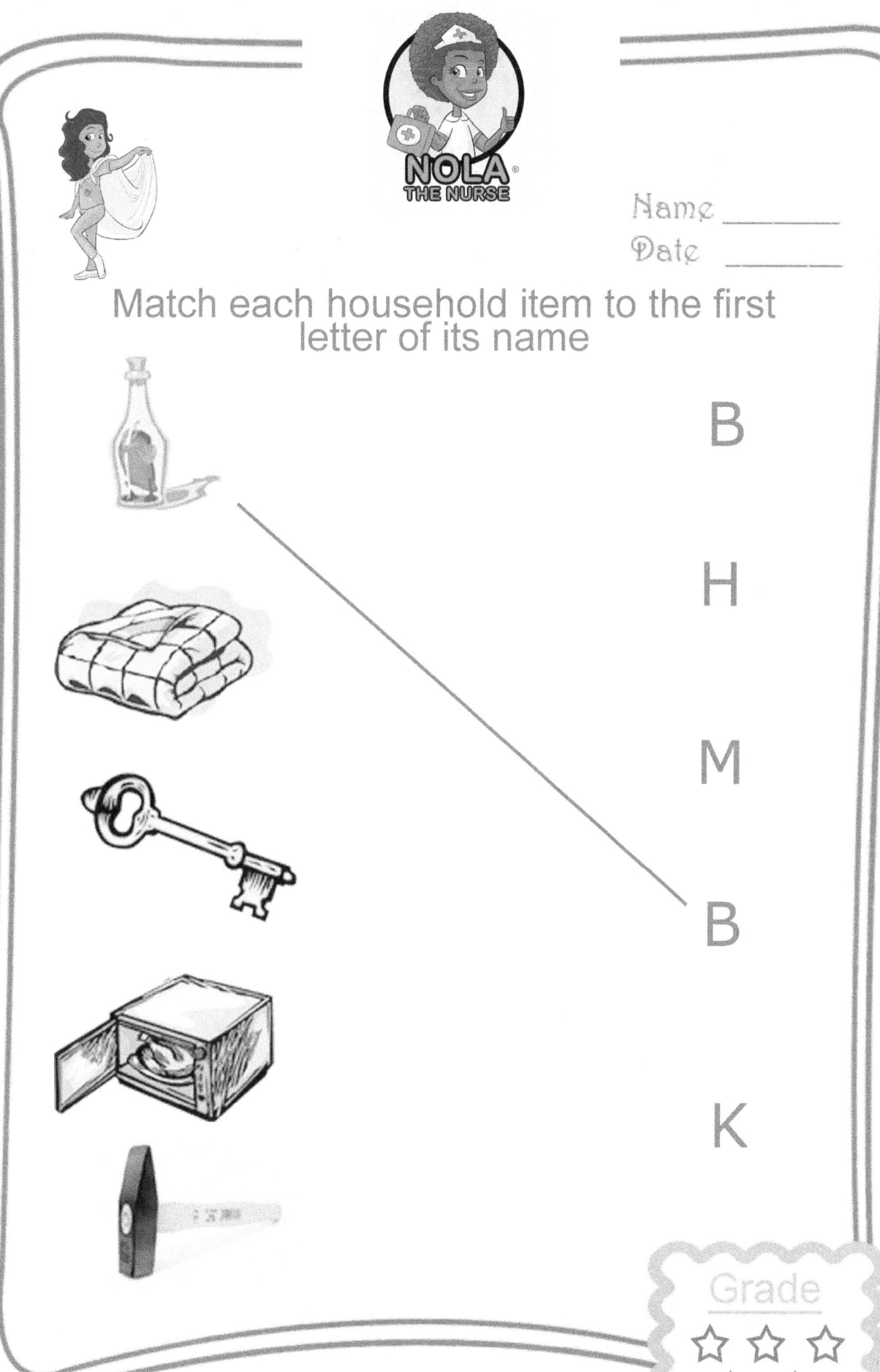

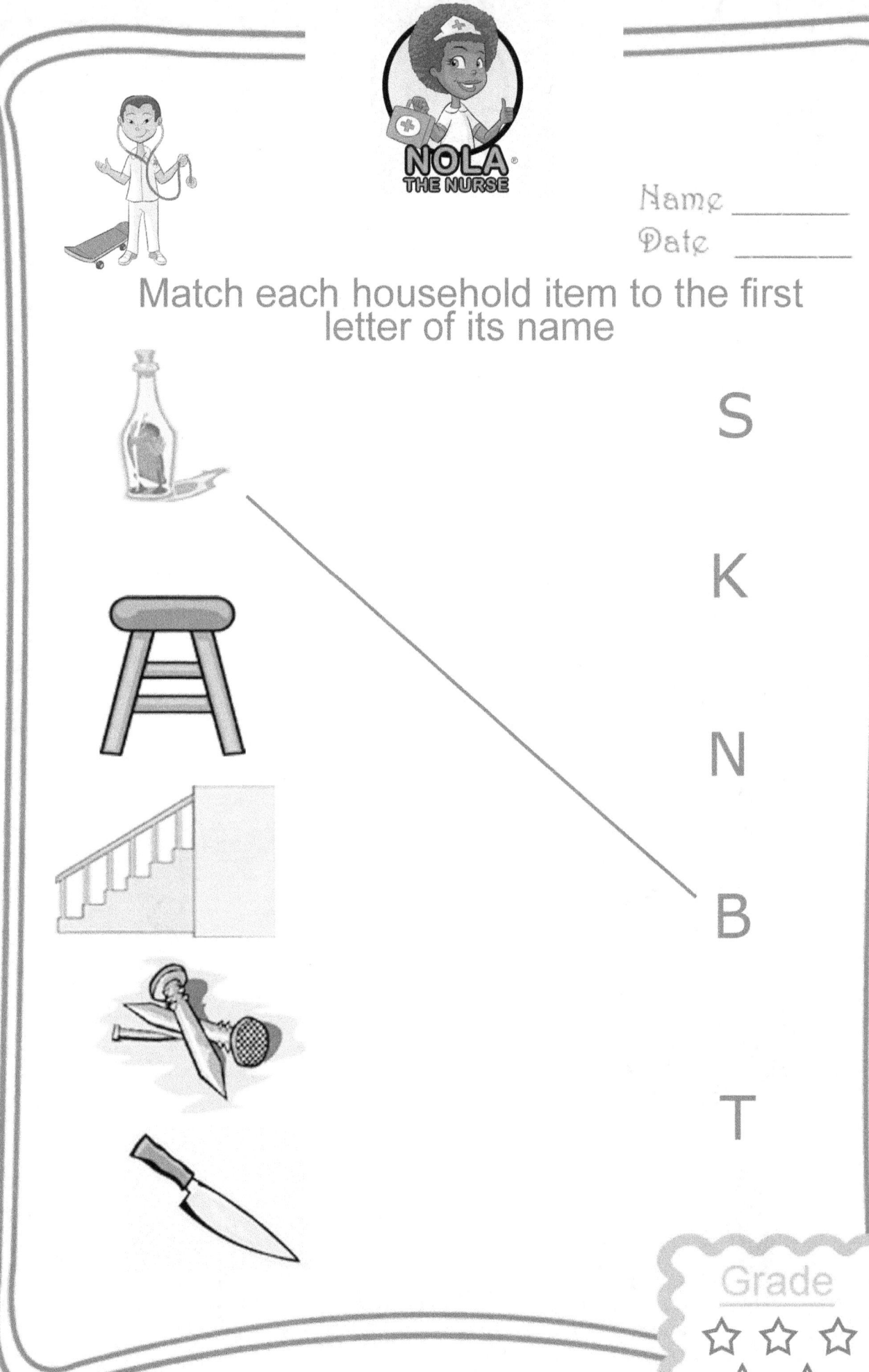

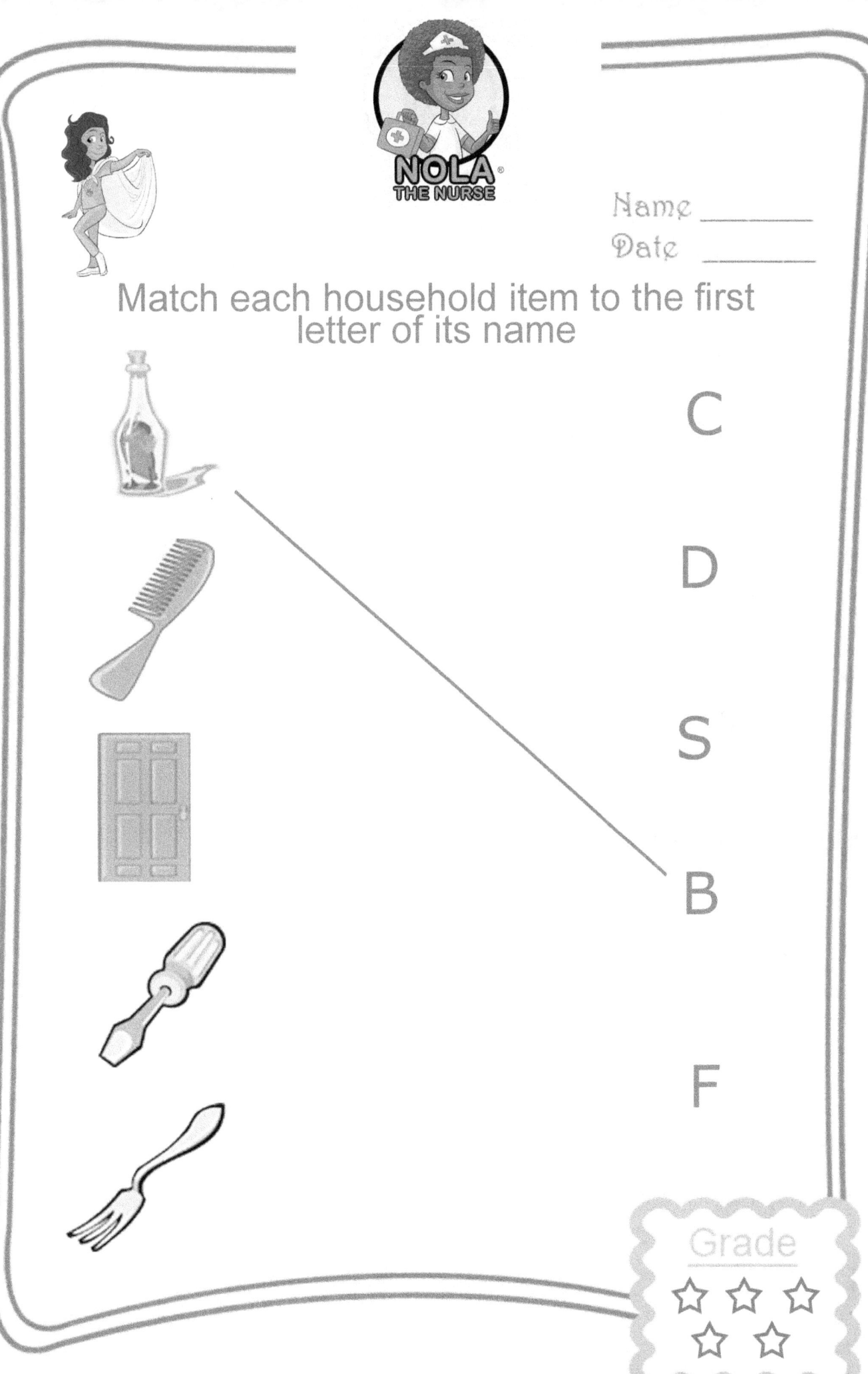

Name _____
Date _____

Match each household item to the first letter of its name

W

L

K

B

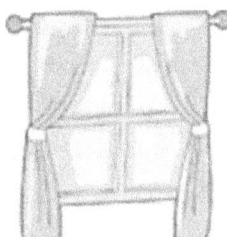

P

Grade

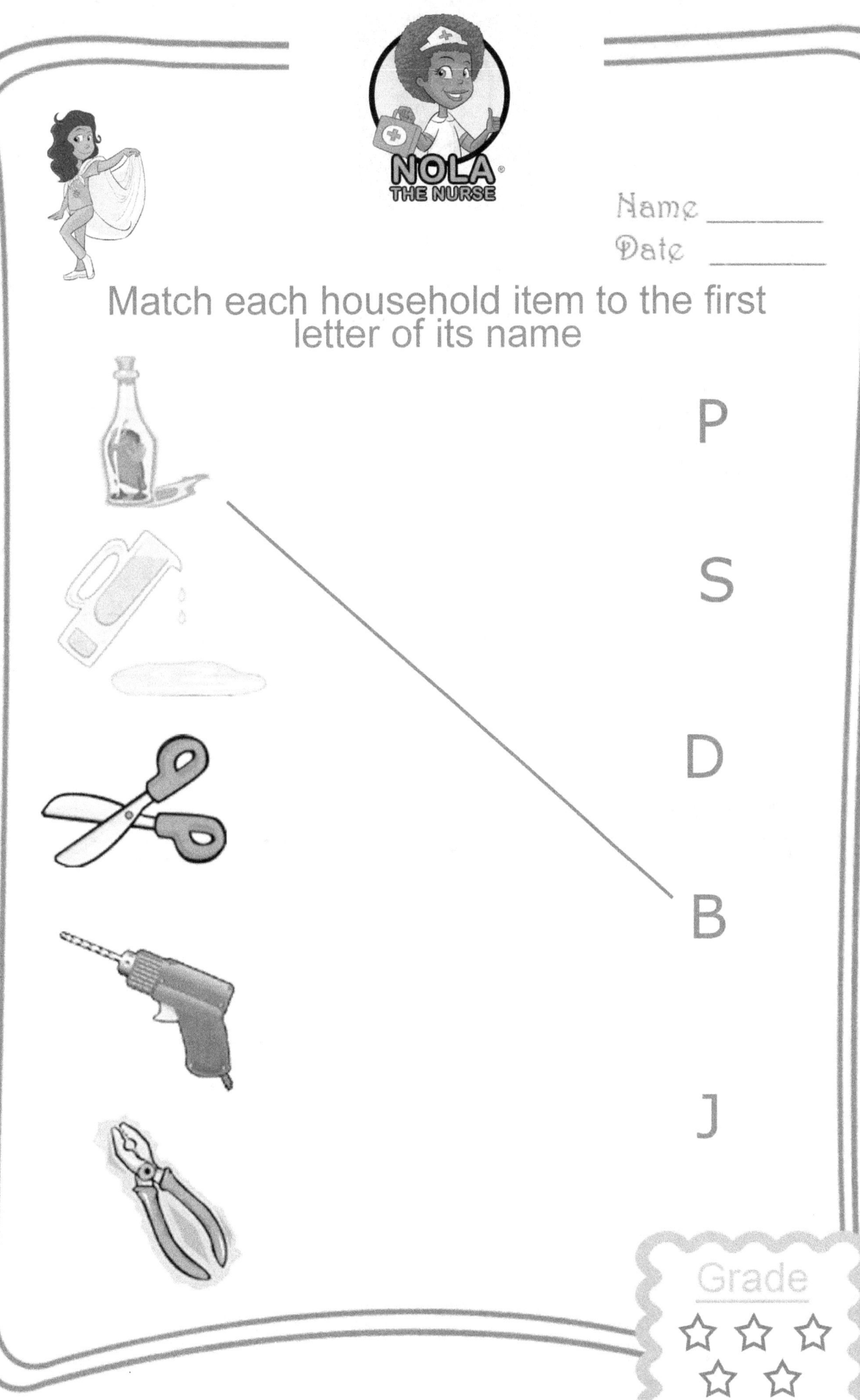

Name _____
Date _____

Write the name of each household item on the line

 bed _____

 bottle _____

 broom _____

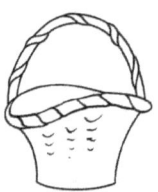 basket _____

Grade

Name _____
Date _____

Write the name of each household item on the line

 tap _____

 bed _____

 bucket _____

 chair _____

Grade

Name _____
Date _____

Write the name of each household item on the line

 brush ----------------

 bucket ----------------

 cabinet ----------------

camera ----------------

Grade

Name _____
Date _____

Write the name of each household item on the line

 candle ----------------

 chair ----------------

 clock ----------------

 comb ----------------

Grade

Name _____
Date _____

Write the name of each household item on the line

 fork ---------------

 freezer ---------------

 frying pan ---------------

🔨 hammer ---------------

Grade

Name _____
Date _____

Write the name of each household item on the line

 nail _____

 oven _____

 paintbrush _____

pencil _____

Grade

Name _____
Date _____

Write the name of each household item on the line

 jug ---------------

 knife ---------------

 lamp ---------------

 mirror ---------------

Grade

Name _____
Date _____

Write the name of each household item on the line

 screwdriver ----------------

 sofa ----------------

 spoon ----------------

 table ----------------

Grade
☆ ☆ ☆
☆ ☆

Name _____
Date _____

Match each household item to its name

	Pillow
	Bed
	Broom
	Bottle
	Pencil

Grade

Name _____
Date _____

Match each household item to its name

	Sewing machine
	Mirror
	Camera
	Vacuum Cleaner
	Blender

Grade

Name _____
Date _____

Match the Household with their names

		Cabinet
		Frying Pan
		Fridge
		Juicer
		Wheelbarrow

Grade

Name _____
Date _____

Match each household item to its name

	Nail
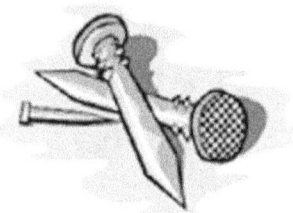	Table
	Tap
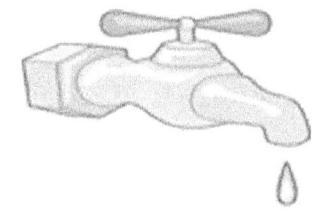	Bathtub
	Sofa

Grade

Name _____
Date _____

Match each household item to its name

	Chair
	Hanger
	Knife
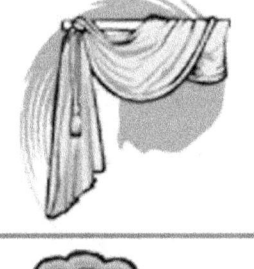	Dustpan
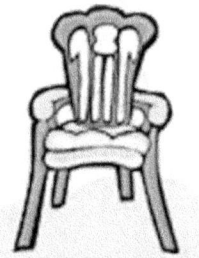	Curtain

Grade

Name _____
Date _____

Match each household item to its name

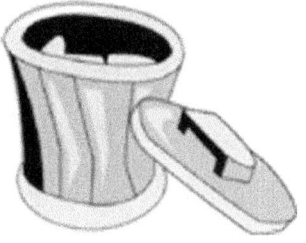		Vase
		Basket
		Candle
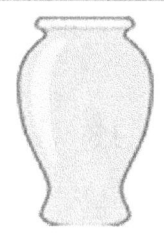		Trash can
		Spoon

Grade

Name _____
Date _____

Match each household item to its name

	Hammer
	Bucket
	Key
	Blanket
	Microwave

Grade

Name _____
Date _____

Match each household item to its name

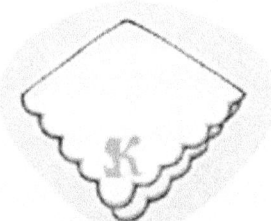	Stairs
	Safety pin
	Toothpaste
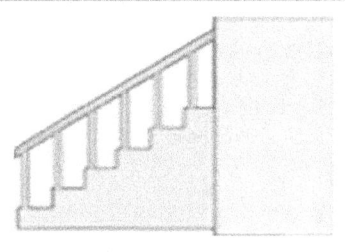	Tissue
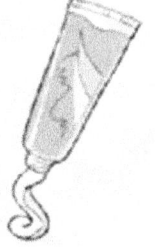	Stool

Grade

Name _____
Date _____

Match each household item to its name

   Fork

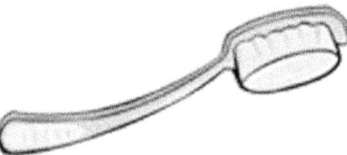   Door

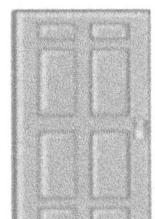   Screwdriver

   Comb

   Toothbrush

Grade
☆ ☆ ☆
☆ ☆

Name _____
Date _____

Match each household item to its name

	Lock
	Plate
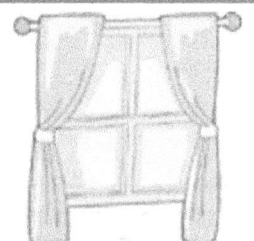	Lamp
	Kitchen
	Window

Grade

Name _____
Date _____

Write the name of each mode of transportation on the line

 car ---------------

 jeep ---------------

 bike ---------------

van ---------------

Grade

Name ____
Date ____

Write the name of each mode of transportation on the line

   tractor   ---------------

   boat   ---------------

   ship   ---------------

   bus   ---------------

Grade

Name _____
Date _____

Match each mode of transportation to its name

	Bus
	Train
	Jeep
	Boat
	Car

Grade
☆ ☆ ☆
☆ ☆

Name _____
Date _____

Match each mode of transportation to its name

Bicycle

Scooter

Tractor

Train

Van

Grade

Name _____
Date _____

Match each mode of transportation to its name

	Motorcycle
	Helicopter
	Ship
	Car
	Tank

Grade

Name _____
Date _____

Match each mode of transportation to its name

	Crane
	Train
	Jeep
	Ambulance
	Truck

Grade

Name _____
Date _____

Match each fruit or vegetable to its name

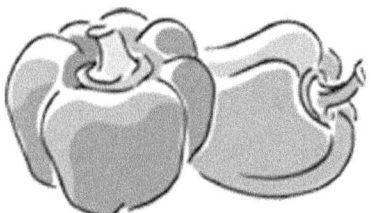	Onion
	Chilli
	Carrot
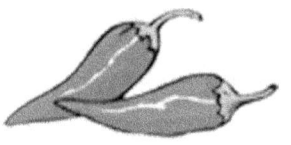	Bellpepper
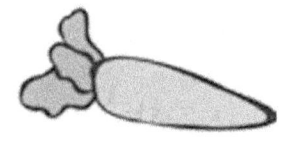	Limes and Lemons

Grade

Match each fruit or vegetable to its name

Name _____
Date _____

 (cabbage)	Tomato
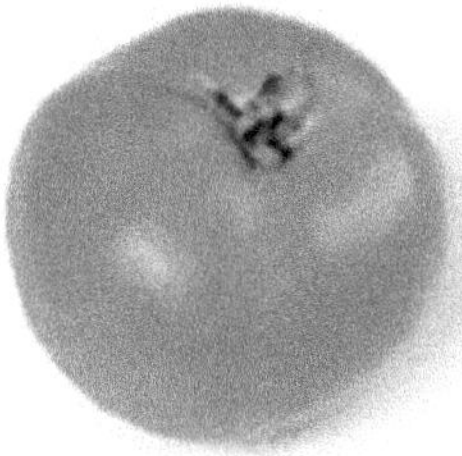 (tomato)	Corn
 (cucumbers)	Pumpkin
 (pumpkin)	Lettuce
 (corn)	Cucumber

Grade

Name _____
Date _____

Match each vegetable to its name

		Garlic
		Cabbage
		Potato
		Eggplant
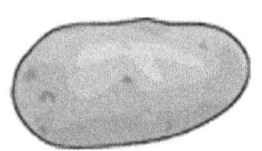		Radish

Grade

Name _____
Date _____

Match each vegetable to its name

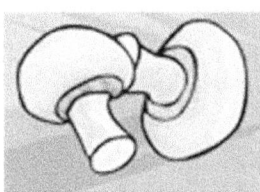	Chilli
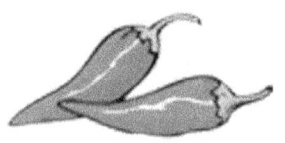	Beans
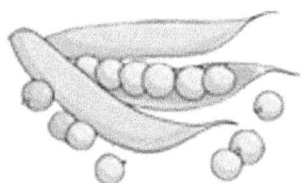	Peas
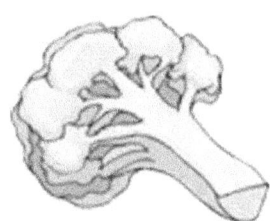	Mushrooms
	Broccoli

Name _____
Date _____

Match each animal to its name

 Elephant

 Camel

 Deer

 Lion

 Fox

Grade

Name _____
Date _____

Match each animal to its name

Rabbit

Crocodile

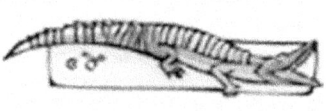

Gorilla

Giraffe

Horse

Grade

Name _____
Date _____

Match each animal to its name

   Hyena

   Wolf

   Hippo

   Dolphin

   Kangaroo

Grade

Name _____
Date _____

Match each animal to its name

	Hyena
	Wolf
	Dog
	Dolphin
	Sheep

Grade
☆ ☆ ☆
☆ ☆

Name _____
Date _____

Match the birds with their names

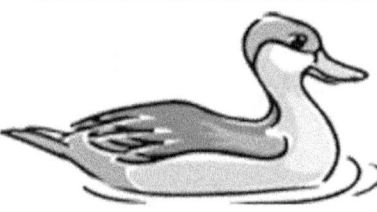

Hen

Eagle

Crow

Crane

Duck

Grade

Name _____
Date _____

Match the birds with their names

	Owl
	Parrot
	Pigeon
	Duck
	Peacock

Grade

Name _____
Date _____

Match the birds with their names

	Sparrow
	Swan
	Penguin
	Woodpecker
	Robin

Name _____
Date _____

Circle the Pictures that begin with the letter of A.

Name _____
Date _____

Circle the Pictures that begin with the letter of B.

  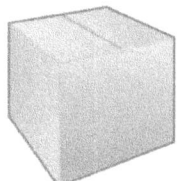

Grade
☆ ☆ ☆
☆ ☆

Name _____
Date _____

Circle the Pictures that begin with the letter of C.

 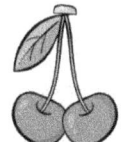 

Name _____
Date _____

Circle the Pictures that begin with the letter of D.

Name _____
Date _____

Circle the Pictures that begin with the letter of E.

Grade

Name _____
Date _____

Circle the Pictures that begin with the letter of F.

 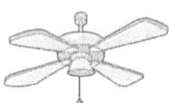 

  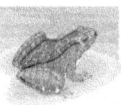

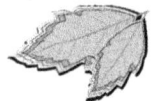  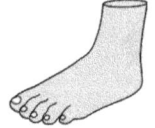

Grade

Name _____
Date _____

Circle the Pictures that begin with the letter of G.

Grade

Name _____
Date _____

Circle the Pictures that begin with the letter of H.

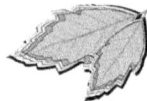

Name _____
Date _____

Circle the Pictures that begin with the letter of I.

 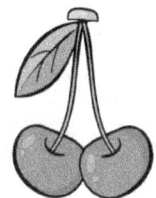 

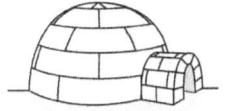  

Name _____
Date _____

Circle the Pictures that begin with the letter of J.

 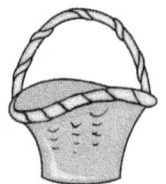 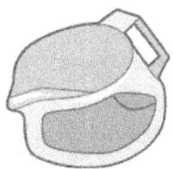

 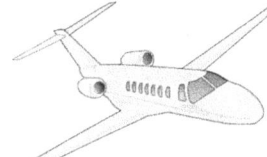 

Name _____
Date _____

Circle the Pictures that begin with the letter of K.

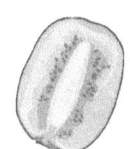

Grade

Name _____
Date _____

Circle the Pictures that begin with the letter of L.

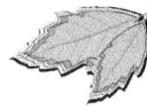

Name _____
Date _____

Circle the Pictures that begin with the letter of M.

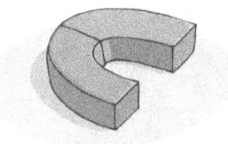

Grade

Name _____
Date _____

Circle the Pictures that begin with the letter of N.

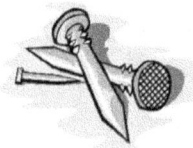

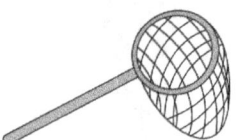

Grade
☆ ☆ ☆
☆ ☆

Name _____
Date _____

Circle the Pictures that begin with the letter of O.

Grade

Name _____
Date _____

Circle the Pictures that begin with the letter of P.

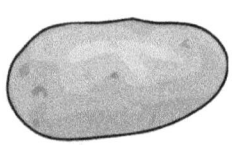

Name _____
Date _____

Circle the Pictures that begin with the letter of Q.

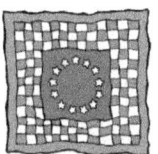

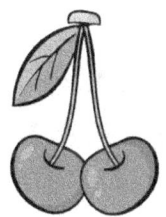

Grade

Name _____
Date _____

Circle the Pictures that begin with the letter of R.

Name _____
Date _____

Circle the Pictures that begin with the letter of S.

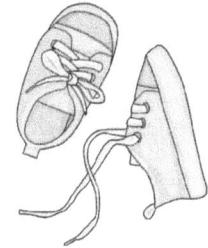

Name _____
Date _____

Circle the Pictures that begin with the letter of T.

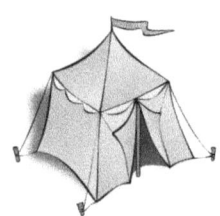 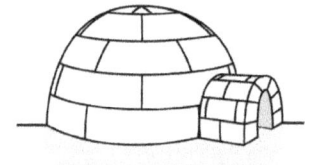 

 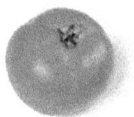 

Name _____
Date _____

Circle the Pictures that begin with the letter of U.

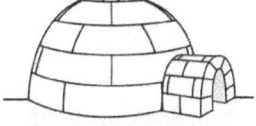
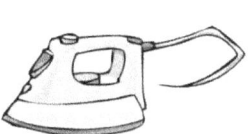

Grade

Circle the Pictures that begin with the letter of V.

Name _____
Date _____

Circle the Pictures that begin with the letter of W.

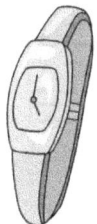

Grade

Name _____
Date _____

Circle the Pictures that begin with the letter of X.

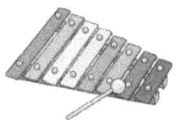

Grade

Name _____
Date _____

Circle the Pictures that begin with the letter of Y.

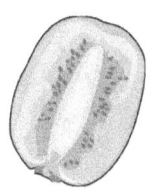

Grade

Name _____
Date _____

Circle the Pictures that begin with the letter of Z.

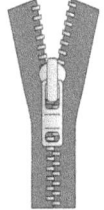

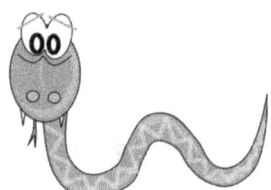

Grade

Name ____
Date ____

Write the last letter of Each Word

co

ca

fis

he

bea

Grade

Name _____
Date _____

Write the last letter of Each Word

orang_____

pea_____

pineappl_____

strawberr_____

watermelo_____

Grade

Name _____
Date _____

Write the last letter of Each Word

 bell peppe____

 broccol____

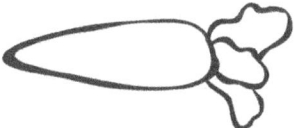 carro____

 cucumbe____

 garli____

Name ____
Date ____

Write the last letter of Each Word

lemo

mushroo

onio

pe

tomat

Grade

Name _____
Date _____

Write the last letter of Each Word

 broccol____

 mushroo____

 carro____

 potat____

 garli____

Grade

Name _____
Date _____

Write the last letter of Each Word

knif

ju

camer

cu

candl

Grade

Name _____
Date _____

Write the last letter of Each Word

   ta

   nai

   violi

   tabl

   penci

Name _____
Date _____

Write the last letter of Each Word

pi

lio

tige

airplan

bik

Grade

Name ___
Date ___

Write the last letter of Each Word

va

jee

ca

tracto

bicycl

Grade

Name _____
Date _____

Write the last letter of Each Word

truc

trai

scoote

bu

shi

Grade

Name _____
Date _____

Write the last letter of Each Word

 be

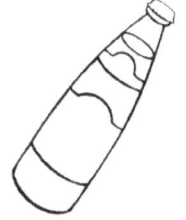 bottl

 broo

 brus

 hamme

Grade

Name _____
Date _____

Write the last letter of Each Word

bucke

doo

chai

drit

cloc

Grade

Name _____
Date _____

Write the last letter of Each Word

_____ cran

_____ duc

_____ eagl

_____ parro

_____ crocodil

Grade

Name _____
Date _____

Write the last letter of Each Word

__pigeo__

__swa__

__sparro__

__duc__

__woodpecke__

Grade

Name _____
Date _____

Write the last letter of Each Word

appl

cherr

cor

grape

banan

Grade

Name _____
Date _____

Write the name of each vegetable on the line

 broccoli ---------------

 carrot ---------------

 lemon ---------------

 bellpeppers ---------------

Grade
☆ ☆ ☆
☆ ☆

Name _____
Date _____

Write the name of each vegetable on the line

 garlic   ----------------

 mushroom ----------------

 radish   ----------------

 onion   ----------------

Name _____
Date _____

Write the name of each vegetable on the line

 cucumber ----------------

 tomato ----------------

 pea ----------------

 potato ----------------

Grade
☆ ☆ ☆
☆ ☆

These following free color sheets are placed here to help you get to know the characters from the Nola The Nurse® children's book series. Enjoy and pick up a copy of the hottest selling children's book in America that was recently featured on The Harry Show!

Dr. Eden Nurse Practitioner

Gumbo

Dr. Baker Nurse Practitioner

Charo The CRNA

Maddi the Midwife

Nola the Nurse Maddi the Midwife Bax the Nurse Charo the CRNA

More books by Dr. Baker

Nola The Nurse® She's On The Go Series Vol 1
Nola The Nurse® & Friends Explore The Holi Fest She's On The Go Series Vol 2
Nola The Nurse® & Friends Explore The Holi Fest She's On The Go Series Vol 2 Coloring Book
Nola The Nurse® Remembers Hurricane Katrina Special Edition
Nola The Nurse® Remembers Hurricane Katrina Special Edition Coloring Book
Black Dot
Nola The Nurse® Math Worksheets for Kindergarten Vol 3
Nola The Nurse® Activity Book for Kindergarten Vol 2
Nola The Nurse® Preschool Activity Book Vol 1

Upcoming Titles:

Nola The Nurse® Math/English Worksheets for Preschoolers Vol 5
Nola The Nurse® Math Worksheets for First Graders Vol 6
Nola The Nurse® STEM Activity Book for 5-8 year olds Vol 7

www.NolaTheNurse.com
DrBaker@NolaTheNurse.com

About the Author

Dr. Scharmaine L. Baker, NP is a nationally recognized and award-winning nurse practitioner in New Orleans, Louisiana. She has received numerous honors and awards for her contributions to healthcare in New Orleans since she became a family nurse practitioner in 2000, including the 2013 Healthcare Hero award (New Orleans City Business magazine) and 2008 Entrepreneur of the Year award (ADVANCE for Nurse Practitioner magazine).

Dr. Baker has a doctor of nursing practice (DNP) degree from Chatham University in Pittsburgh, PA, and she is a fellow of the American Association of Nurse Practitioners (AANP). She was inspired to make house calls while caring for her grandmother, who was ill and needed an in-home doctor.

After Hurricane Katrina, Dr. Baker was instrumental in caring for the sick and disabled in New Orleans, where hospitals had closed and doctors had evacuated but never returned. Her patient load went from 100 to 500 in only three months. Thanks to her passion and unwavering dedication to caring for homebound patients in her home town, Dr. Baker's story was featured on the CBS Evening News with Katie Couric.

Today, Dr. Baker maintains a busy private practice in New Orleans by making house calls to the elderly and disabled who would otherwise not receive healthcare.

When this award-winning and nationally known nurse practitioner is not on the road delivering keynote speeches and attending various other media events, she loves reading to her children, Skylar Rose and Wyatt Shane.

www.DrBakerNP.com
www.NolaTheNurse.com
https://shop.nolathenurse.com

www.ingramcontent.com/pod-product-compliance
Lightning Source LLC
Chambersburg PA
CBHW081344080526
44588CB00016B/2371